TEACHING PHYSICAL EDUCATION CREATIVELY

D0552471

Teaching Physical Education Creatively provides knowledge and understanding in order to engage creatively with the primary Physical Education curriculum for both trainee teachers and qualified teachers. It is full of ideas for developing the teaching of dance, games, gymnastics, and outdoor and adventurous activities in an innovative and engaging manner.

With an emphasis on developing creative teaching processes by building from children's curiosity, imagination and need to explore and move, it forges clear links between research and practice, and offers suggestions for developing exciting, engaging new approaches to teaching Physical Education.

Key topics explored include:

- physical competence and physical literacy
- creative ways to develop the teaching of dance, games, gymnastics, and outdoor and adventurous activities
- developing understanding of space, speed and dynamics
- creative lesson planning
- inclusive approaches and aspects of differentiation

Teaching Physical Education Creatively presents the theory and background necessary to develop a comprehensive understanding of creative teaching and children's learning. Packed with practical guidance and inspiration for lively, enjoyable Physical Education, it is an invaluable resource for undergraduate and postgraduate students in initial teacher training, practising teachers and undergraduate students of Physical Education.

Angela Pickard is Editor in Chief for the *Research in Dance Education* journal and Programme Director for Dance Education and Dance at Canterbury Christ Church University, UK.

Patricia Maude is College Tutor at Homerton College, University of Cambridge, UK.

OXFORD BROOKES
UNIVERSITY
LIBRARY

00 975026 02

THE LEARNING TO TEACH IN THE PRIMARY SCHOOL SERIES

Series editor: Teresa Cremin, The Open University, UK

Teaching is an art form. It demands not only knowledge and understanding of the core areas of learning, but also the ability to teach these creatively and foster learner creativity in the process. *The Learning to Teach in the Primary School Series* draws upon recent research that indicates the rich potential of creative teaching and learning, and explores what it means to teach creatively in the primary phase. It also responds to the evolving nature of subject teaching in a wider, more imaginatively framed twenty-first-century primary curriculum.

Designed to complement the textbook *Learning to Teach in the Primary School*, the well-informed, lively texts offer support for students and practising teachers who want to develop more creative approaches to teaching and learning. The books highlight the importance of the teachers' own creative engagement, and share a wealth of innovative ideas to enrich pedagogy and practice.

Titles in the series:

Teaching English Creatively
Teresa Cremin

Teaching Science Creatively
Dan Davies

Teaching Mathematics Creatively
Trisha Pound and Linda Lee

Teaching Geography Creatively
Edited by Stephen Scoffham

Teaching History Creatively
Edited by Hilary Cooper

Teaching Music Creatively
Pam Burnard and Regina Murphy

Teaching Physical Education Creatively
Angela Pickard and Patricia Maude

TEACHING PHYSICAL EDUCATION CREATIVELY

Angela Pickard and Patricia Maude

Routledge
Taylor & Francis Group

LONDON AND NEW YORK

First published 2014
by Routledge
2 Park Square, Milton Park, Abingdon, Oxon OX14 4RN

and by Routledge
711 Third Avenue, New York, NY 10017

Routledge is an imprint of the Taylor & Francis Group, an informa business

© 2014 A. Pickard and P. Maude

The right of A. Pickard and P. Maude to be identified as authors of this work has been asserted by them in accordance with sections 77 and 78 of the Copyright, Designs and Patents Act 1988.

All rights reserved. No part of this book may be reprinted or reproduced or utilised in any form or by any electronic, mechanical, or other means, now known or hereafter invented, including photocopying and recording, or in any information storage or retrieval system, without permission in writing from the publishers.

Trademark notice: Product or corporate names may be trademarks or registered trademarks, and are used only for identification and explanation without intent to infringe.

British Library Cataloguing in Publication Data
A catalogue record for this book is available from the British Library

Library of Congress Cataloging in Publication Data
Pickard, Angela.
  Teaching physical education creatively/Angela Pickard, Patricia Maude.
  pages cm
  1. Physical education for children – Study and teaching (Early childhood).
  2. Physical education teachers – Training of. 3. Physical education and training – Curricula. 4. Child development. I. Maude, Patricia. II. Title.
  GV443.P496 2014
  372.86 – dc23
  2013043453

ISBN: 978-0-415-65607-8 (hbk)
ISBN: 978-0-415-65608-5 (pbk)
ISBN: 978-1-315-78035-1 (ebk)

Typeset in Times New Roman and Helvetica Neue
by Florence Production Ltd, Stoodleigh, Devon, UK

ACC. NO. 97502602		FUND El)UG
LOC. ET	CATEGORY I WEEK	PRICE £19.99
29 AUG 2014		
CLASS No. 372.86 PIC		
OXFORD BROOKES UNIVERSITY LIBRARY		

Printed and bound in Great Britain by
TJ International Ltd, Padstow, Cornwall

CONTENTS

SERIES EDITOR'S FOREWORD

Teresa Cremin

Over the last two decades, teachers in England, working in a culture of accountability and target setting, have experienced a high level of specification both of curriculum content and pedagogy. Positioned as recipients of the prescribed agenda, it could be argued that practitioners have had their hands tied, their voices quietened and their professional autonomy constrained. Research reveals that during this time, some professionals have short-changed their understanding of pedagogy and practice (English *et al.* 2002; Burns and Myhill 2004) in order to deliver the required curriculum. The relentless quest for higher standards and 'coverage' may well have obscured the personal and affective dimensions of teaching and learning, fostering a mindset characterised more by compliance and conformity than curiosity and creativity.

However, alongside the standards agenda, creativity and creative policies and practices also became prominent, and a focus on creative teaching and learning developed. Heralded by the publication *All Our Futures: Creativity, Culture and Education* (NACCCE 1999), this shift was exemplified in the Creative Partnerships initiative, in the Qualifications and Curriculum Authority's creativity framework (QCA 2005) and in a plethora of reports (e.g. DfES 2003; Ofsted 2003; CapeUK 2006; Roberts 2006). It was also evident in the development of the Curriculum for Excellence in Scotland. The definition of creativity frequently employed was that creativity is 'imaginative activity fashioned so as to produce outcomes that are both original and of value' (NACCCE 1999: 30). Many schools sought to develop more innovative curricula, and many teachers found renewed energy through teaching creatively and teaching for creativity.

Yet tensions persist, not only because the dual policies of performativity and creativity appear contradictory, but also because the new National Curriculum draft programmes of study in England at least afford a high degree of specificity and profile the knowledge needed to be taught and tested. We need to be concerned if teachers are positioned more as technically competent curriculum deliverers, rather than artistically engaged, research-informed curriculum developers. I believe, alongside Eisner (2003) and others, that teaching is an art form and that teachers benefit from viewing themselves as versatile artists in the classroom, drawing on their personal passions and creativity as they research and develop practice. As Joubert observes:

> Creative teaching is an art. One cannot teach teachers didactically how to be creative; there is no fail-safe recipe or routines. Some strategies may help to promote creative thinking, but teachers need to develop a full repertoire of skills which they can adapt to different situations.
>
> (Joubert 2001: 21)

However, creative teaching is only part of the picture, since teaching for creativity also needs to be acknowledged, and their mutual dependency recognised. The former focuses more on teachers using imaginative approaches in the classroom in order to make learning more interesting and effective; the latter more on the development of children's creativity (NACCCE 1999). Both rely upon an understanding of the notion of creativity and demand that professionals confront the myths and mantras that surround the word. These include the commonly held misconceptions that creativity is connected only to participation in the arts and that it is confined to particular individuals, a competence of a few specially gifted children.

Nonetheless, creativity is an elusive concept; it has been multiply defined by educationalists, psychologists and neurologists, as well as by policymakers in different countries and cultural contexts. Debates resound about its individual and/or collaborative nature, the degree to which it is generic or domain specific, and the difference between the 'Big C' creativity of genius and the 'little c' creativity of the everyday. Notwithstanding these issues, most scholars in the field perceive that it involves the capacity to generate, reason and critically evaluate novel ideas and/or imaginary scenarios. As such, I perceive that it encompasses thinking through and solving problems, making connections, inventing and reinventing, and flexing one's imaginative muscles in all aspects of learning and life.

In the primary classroom, creative teaching and learning have been associated with innovation, originality, ownership and control (Jeffrey and Woods 2009), and creative teachers have been seen, in their planning and teaching, and in the ethos that they create, to afford high value to curiosity and risk-taking, to ownership, autonomy and making connections (Cremin 2009; Cremin et al. 2009). Such teachers, it has been posited, often work in partnership with others: with children, other teachers and experts from beyond the school gates (Cochrane and Cockett 2007). Additionally, in research exploring possibility thinking, which, it is argued, is at the heart of creativity in education (Craft 2000), an intriguing interplay between teachers and children has been observed; both are involved in possibility thinking their ways forwards and in immersing themselves in playful contexts, posing questions, being imaginative, showing self-determination, taking risks and innovating (Burnard et al. 2006; Cremin et al. 2006; Craft et al. 2012). A new pedagogy of possibility beckons.

The Learning to Teach in the Primary School Series, which accompanies and complements the edited textbook Learning to Teach in the Primary School (Arthur and Cremin 2010), seeks to support teachers in developing as creative practitioners, assisting them in exploring the synergies and potential of teaching creatively and teaching for creativity. The series does not merely offer practical strategies for use in the classroom, though these abound, but more importantly seeks to widen teachers' and student teachers' knowledge and understanding of the principles underpinning a creative approach to teaching. Principles based on research. It seeks to mediate the wealth of research evidence, and make accessible and engaging the diverse theoretical perspectives and scholarly arguments available, demonstrating their practical relevance and value to the profession. Those who aspire to develop further as creative and curious educators will, I trust, find much of value to support their own professional learning journeys, and enrich their pedagogy and practice and children's creative learning right across the curriculum.

ABOUT THE SERIES EDITOR

Teresa Cremin (Grainger) is a Professor of Education (Literacy) at the Open University and a past President of UKRA (2001–2002) and UKLA (2007–2009). She is currently Co-Convenor of the BERA Creativity SIG and a Trustee of Booktrust, the Poetry Archive and UKLA. She is also a Fellow of the English Association and an Academician of the Academy of Social Sciences. Her work involves research, publication and consultancy in literacy and creativity. Her current projects seek to explore children's make-believe play in the context of storytelling and storyacting, their everyday lives and literacy practices, and the nature of literary discussions in extracurricular reading groups. Additionally, Teresa is interested in teachers' identities as readers and writers, and the characteristics and associated pedagogy that foster possibility thinking within creative learning in the primary years. Teresa has published widely, writing and co-editing a variety of books, including: *Writing Voices: Creating Communities of Writers* (Routledge, 2012); *Teaching English Creatively* (Routledge, 2009); *Learning to Teach in the Primary School* (Routledge, 2010); *Jumpstart Drama* (David Fulton, 2009); *Documenting Creative Learning 5–11* (Trentham, 2007); *Creativity and Writing: Developing Voice and Verve* (Routledge, 2005); *Teaching English in Higher Education* (NATE and UKLA, 2007); *Creative Activities for Character, Setting and Plot, 5–7, 7–9, 9–11* (Scholastic, 2004); and *Language and Literacy: A Routledge Reader* (Routledge, 2001).

REFERENCES

Arthur, J. and Cremin, T. (2010) (eds) *Learning to Teach in the Primary School* (second edition), London: Routledge.

Burnard, P., Craft, A. and Cremin, T. (2006) 'Possibility thinking', *International Journal of Early Years Education*, 14(3): 243–62.

Burns, C. and Myhill, D. (2004) 'Interactive or inactive? A consideration of the nature of interaction in whole class teaching', *Cambridge Journal of Education*, 34: 35–49.

CapeUK (2006) *Building Creative Futures: The Story of Creative Action Research Awards, 2004–2005*, London: Arts Council.

Cochrane, P. and Cockett, M. (2007) *Building a Creative School: A Dynamic Approach to School Development*, London: Trentham.

Craft, A. (2000) *Creativity Across the Primary Curriculum*, London: Routledge.

Craft, A., McConnon, L. and Mathews, A. (2012) 'Creativity and child-initiated play', *Thinking Skills and Creativity*, 7(1): 48–61.

Cremin, T. (2009) 'Creative teaching and creative teachers', in A. Wilson (ed.), *Creativity in Primary Education*, Exeter: Learning Matters, pp. 36–46.

Cremin, T., Burnard, P. and Craft, A. (2006) 'Pedagogy and possibility thinking in the early years', *International Journal of Thinking Skills and Creativity*, 1(2): 108–19.

Cremin, T., Barnes, J. and Scoffham, S. (2009) *Creative Teaching for Tomorrow: Fostering a Creative State of Mind*, Deal: Future Creative.

Department for Education and Skills (DfES) (2003) *Excellence and Enjoyment: A Strategy for Primary Schools*, Nottingham: DfES.

Eisner, E. (2003) 'Artistry in education', *Scandinavian Journal of Educational Research*, 47(3): 373–84.

English, E., Hargreaves, L. and Hislam, J. (2002) 'Pedagogical dilemmas in the National Literacy Strategy: primary teachers' perceptions, reflections and classroom behaviour', *Cambridge Journal of Education*, 32(1): 9–26.

Jeffrey, B. and Woods, P. (2009) *Creative Learning in the Primary School*, London: Routledge.

Joubert, M. M. (2001) 'The art of creative teaching: NACCCE and beyond', in A. Craft, B. Jeffrey and M. Liebling (eds), *Creativity in Education*, London: Continuum.

National Advisory Committee on Creative and Cultural Education (NACCCE) (1999) *All Our Futures: Creativity, Culture and Education*, London: Department for Education and Employment.

Ofsted (2003) *Expecting the Unexpected: Developing Creativity in Primary and Secondary Schools*, HMI 1612, available at: www.ofsted.gov.uk (accessed 9 November 2007).

Qualifications and Curriculum Authority (QCA) (2005) *Creativity: Find it, Promote it! Promoting Pupils' Creative Thinking and Behaviour Across the Curriculum at Key Stages 1, 2 and 3 – Practical Materials for Schools*, London: QCA.

Roberts, P. (2006) *Nurturing Creativity in Young People. A Report to Government to Inform Future Policy*, London: DCMS.

ACKNOWLEDGEMENTS

Special thanks to the following for their generous support in providing for the photographs:

The headteacher, staff and children at Dubai Gem School, Dubai, UAE
The headteacher, staff and children at Hardwick Primary School, Cambridgeshire
The headteacher, staff and children at Milton Road Primary School, Cambridge
The coaches and gymnasts at Homerton and Netherhall Gymnastics Clubs, Cambridge

and to Zachary des Ruisseau for his part in preparing and taking some of the photographs.

TEACHING PHYSICAL EDUCATION CREATIVELY

INTRODUCTION

In this book, we argue that teaching is itself a creative act and that learning is a creative activity; a process of exploration, discovery, problem-solving, ways of representing knowledge, experience and thinking in a variety of ways. We are concerned with how creative processes can be harnessed by every teacher and every learner within Physical Education. It is an aim of this book to encourage and enable teachers to fully engage with a creative approach to the teaching of Physical Education in the primary phase. In order to support teaching for creativity, we draw on five key principles that underpin teaching Physical Education creatively, which are outlined and discussed later in this chapter. These core features are at the heart of our thinking as we explore and share examples of creative learning and teaching approaches in this book within specific areas of the Physical Education curriculum. It is hoped that this book will also demonstrate starting points for you to develop further creative learning and teaching opportunities in Physical Education. This chapter contends that Physical Education has valuable purposes as a means to develop physical, intellectual, emotional, social and artistic capabilities. We introduce and argue for creativity, explore the range of policy, practice and definitions that exist in relation to creativity, consider creative teaching and teaching for creativity, and outline the creative potential of the body through the core features of teaching for creativity.

This book is well timed because, at the time of writing, a review of the Primary National Curriculum has just been completed; the draft Physical Education programme of study was published in September 2013 and is to be introduced for teaching into schools by September 2014. It is worth noting that criticisms of the previous National Curriculum claimed that it was 'squeezing out room for innovation, creativity, deep learning and intellectual exploration' (DfE 2010: 40). Within the report regarding the National Curriculum review, it has been suggested that:

> Schools should be given greater freedom over the curriculum. The National Curriculum should set out only the essential knowledge (facts, concepts, principles and fundamental operations) that all children should acquire, and leave schools to design a wider school curriculum that best meets the needs of their pupils and to decide how to teach this most effectively.
>
> (DfE 2011: 6)

Furthermore, Children's Minister Tim Loughton, in his speech 'Promoting PE in schools', which he gave to the Association of Physical Education, claimed that:

> Although we are clear we want PE, swimming and competitive sport to be a compulsory part of the curriculum at each of the four key stages, the new Programme of Study, when it comes out, will be shorter, simpler and far less prescriptive to allow for the maximum level of innovation in schools . . . in return we need you to seize the opportunity to be creative, to inspire young people to engage with PE and help them understand the enormous benefits it offers.
>
> (Loughton 2012)

Teaching and learning in Physical Education should be rich, inspiring, purposeful and imaginative.

A Health Position Paper in 2008 from Association for Physical Education (AfPE) shared a useful definition of Physical Education:

> Physical Education is the planned, progressive, inclusive learning experiences that take place as part of the curriculum and acts as the foundation for a lifelong engagement in physical activity and sport. The learning experiences offered to children should be developmentally appropriate to help them acquire psychomotor skills, cognitive understanding, social skills and the emotional learning they need to lead a physically active life.
>
> (Harris 2008: 3)

Physical Education has lifelong value and purpose and lends itself to a creative approach to learning and teaching. Much research has found the multiple benefits of a creative approach to learning and teaching (Fryer 1996; Beetlestone 1998; Gough 1999; Sternberg 1999; Craft 2000; Craft et al. 2001; Jeffrey and Woods 2003; Fisher and Williams 2004; Craft 2005; Jeffrey 2005; Jeffrey 2006). Such an approach means teaching essential knowledge, skills and understanding within creative contexts where the focus is on developing children's capacity to become highly active explorers of knowledge, ideas and strategies, and in enabling and motivating them to apply knowledge and skills by making choices and decisions. High-quality and creative teachers offer a careful balance of support and challenge to learners in order to enable them to explore their capabilities with confidence and to extend their abilities to work effectively in all aspects of Physical Education. As Desailly (2012: 3), drawing on Jeffrey and Craft (2001), contends, 'there is a strong argument that creative teaching is actually effective teaching'.

WHAT IS CREATIVITY?

There has been much debate about this illusive term 'creativity'. Creativity is typically described in terms of a product, a process or a creative person (Mooney 1963; Taylor 1998; Lubart 1999), and can be seen as reflected in everyday potential as opposed to being preserved for the gifted few. Creativity, then, involves ideas, playfulness, exploration, problem-solving, purposefulness, and artistic and imaginative invention. Anna Craft (2001, 2002) uses the phrase 'little c creativity', which values 'everyday' or ordinary creativity, in contrast to extraordinary or 'big c' creativity:

Little c creativity . . . focuses on the resourcefulness and agency of ordinary people. A 'democratic' notion, in that I propose it can be manifested by anyone (and not just a few). It refers to ability to route-find, successfully charting new courses through everyday challenges. It is the sort of creativity, or 'agency' which guides route finding and choices in everyday life. It involves being imaginative, being original/innovative, stepping at times outside of convention, going beyond the obvious, being self-aware of all of this in taking active, conscious, and intentional action in the world.

(Craft 2002: 56)

The *All Our Futures: Creativity, Culture and Education* report (NACCCE 1999) was significant as it recommended a core role for creativity in relation to both learning and pedagogy. The encouragement was for greater creativity in education through 'a balance between teaching skills and understanding and promoting the freedom to innovate and take risks' (NACCCE 1999: 10). Here, creativity was defined as 'imaginative activity fashioned so as to produce outcomes that are both original and of value' (NACCCE 1999: 29). A definition of creativity dependent on end products does limit its potential, so this book engages with creative processes; the generation of creative ideas, creative responses, creative composition, creative appreciation and evaluation.

A number of policies and practices promoting creativity in schools followed the NACCCE (1999) report, all influenced by political and economic agendas. These included *Excellence and Enjoyment* (DfES 2003), *Expecting the Unexpected: Developing Creativity in Primary and Secondary Schools* (Ofsted 2003), *Creativity: Find It, Promote It* (QCA 2003), *Creative Partnerships Programme* (DfES 2006), which funded education projects involving community artists, and *Nurturing Creativity in Young People* (DCMS and DfES 2006). An extension of the policy sought to involve young people as both spectators and participants in creativity and culture through the introduction of a five-hours-a-week 'cultural offer' (DCMS and DfES 2007). This policy refocused the Creative Partnerships programme as a cultural learning programme (McMaster 2008), where young people, through partnership, were to 'find their talent' (Creative Partnerships 2008).The Early Years Foundation Stage (DCSF 2008) also recognised the importance of creativity and the role of teachers in fostering children's curiosity and capacity to take risks. Furthermore, in 'Towards a New Curriculum', Alexander (2009) affirmed the need for independent and creative thinkers and learners. Embedded in this arts-and-culture-orientated policy was a notion of creativity as 'life-wide' (Craft 2005).

Despite these developments, and also due to a change in government in 2010, there remains anxiety among educators that creativity is being stifled. Indeed, the focus on creativity has been paralleled by an expansion of performativity policies used by the government to seek to raise standards in schools. The Department for Children, Schools and Families (DCSF), together with the Qualifications and Curriculum Authority (QCA), has now established a significant 'performativity' culture (Evans *et al.* 2005) through national inspections, national testing, target setting and league tables. It has been argued that the creativity/creative learning policy contrasts with the continuing testing regimes, audit culture and quality assurance measures that seem to favour technician-orientated pedagogies (Jeffrey and Woods 1998, 2003; Boyd 2005). It appears that teachers in England are encouraged, on the one hand, to take risks, innovate and nurture creativity, and, on the other hand, are subject to heavy-duty tracking, measurement and accountability. As Cullingford (2007: 133) asserted, creativity represents 'open mindedness, exploration, the celebration of difference and . . . is taken to be an automatic opposition to the language of targets, to instrumental skills, the measurement of outcomes and the dogmas of accountability'. Performativity can be seen to be 'hijacking the creativity discourse' (Turner-Bisset 2007: 201), and this impact has been felt sharply within the foundation subjects. Curriculum time in Physical Education (PE) has become increasingly marginalised as greater emphasis has been placed on teaching core subjects such as Literacy and Mathematics. Nevertheless, creativity within Physical Education is possible within subject-focused time, but also with a range of other subjects in a cross-curricular way. Given the pressure of target setting and a heavy emphasis on coverage that seems to exist in the current curriculum, it is unsurprising that some may think that it is safer to teach in a traditional, didactic manner where learners are viewed as 'empty vessels' (Piaget 1952) as opposed to active builders of knowledge. Desailly (2012: 4) makes a strong argument when she says that 'becoming a teacher who is able to teach creatively and to encourage pupils to learn creatively and to develop their own creativity is also to become a highly effective teacher'. We acknowledge that to teach creatively may take some teachers out of their comfort zone, but, as Goodwin (2010: 10) summarises, there is an excitement as well as a risk in creativity, stating that 'creativity can be uncomfortable, unpredictable, anarchic, boundary breaking and insecure but also playful, invigorating and pleasurable'.

CREATIVE TEACHING AND TEACHING FOR CREATIVITY IN PHYSICAL EDUCATION

Creative teaching, then, can be viewed as 'using imaginative approaches to make learning more interesting and effective' (NACCCE 1999) and the features of creative teaching, as proposed by Craft (2005), could include innovation, relevance and ownership. Central to teaching is the learner, and teaching for creativity can be seen as having a clear intention to develop children's own creative thinking and behaviour (NACCCE 1999). Creativity should not be treated as a temporary fashion; in teaching for creativity, teachers must embrace a willingness and commitment to explore ideas with children and make choices governed by knowledge and expertise, but also to place the needs of the learners at the heart of what they do. Such teachers create relevance and engagement so that *all* the children will *want* to learn. *Teaching for creativity principles*, as suggested by NACCCE (1999), are worthy of some consideration. These are: encouraging young people to believe in their creative identity; identifying young people's creative abilities; fostering creativity by developing some of the common capacities and sensitivities of creativity such as curiosity; recognising and becoming more knowledgeable about the creative processes that help foster creativity development; and providing opportunities to be creative – a hands-on approach. Moreover, the *Ten Key Principles of Effective Teaching and Learning* (James and Pollard 2011) also argue that effective teaching and learning promote the active engagement of the learner.

Children enjoy, engage with and learn from creative teachers, and learn most from teachers who support and challenge their thinking. However, it is important that creativity is not thought to be 'equated with sloppiness' (Desailly 2012: 3). Children do need specific knowledge and skills for their creativity to flourish. As Barnes (2007: 239) suggests, 'the robustness and rigidity of this disciplined understanding can in many ways be the best provoker of creativity'. The NACCCE report makes it clear that in its view, sustained creative development 'involves knowledge of the field in question and skills in the media concerned . . . [and to] recognise the mutual dependence of freedom and control at the heart of the creative process' (NACCCE 1999: paragraph 49). It is important for us to clarify what creativity means to us and how we can put it at the heart of teaching and learning. Cremin (2009) argues that it is possible to adopt a creative mindset or attitude through capacity to generate, reason with and critically evaluate in dealing with the mundane as well as the unusual aspects of everyday life; the creative process can involve risk, challenge, uncertainty and criticality. Creative professionals can combine subject and pedagogical knowledge and teach creatively and teach for creativity.

CREATIVE POTENTIAL OF THE BODY – CORE FEATURES OF TEACHING FOR CREATIVE BODIES

A creative approach to teaching Physical Education enables teachers to make informed decisions in relation to planning, provision, teaching strategies, assessment and evaluation. Such decisions are based on secure and confident subject and pedagogical knowledge and an understanding of the creative potential of the body. Physical Education can:

> develop skills in interaction, team-working, problem-solving, observing, evaluating, verbal and non-verbal communication of ideas and emotions, and in making connections . . . can improve self-esteem and confidence, it can widen aspiration.
>
> (Siddall 2010: 10)

In these ways, Physical Education has the potential to bring to the learner body confidence and power. Using the notion of power, the elements or core features of a creative approach in Physical Education that are examined within the book are introduced here. They are not in a linear order, and have equal value. They are:

- ■ **PURPOSE** – *Valuing purposeful physical exploration and meaning-making.*
- ■ **OPPORTUNITIES** – *Harnessing opportunities within and across the curriculum.*
- ■ **WELL-BEING** – *Developing awareness of health and well-being.*
- ■ **ENVIRONMENT** – *Providing a motivating and inclusive climate.*
- ■ **REVEL** – *Initiating celebration of physical success, achievement and progression.*

Over the last decade, there has been a plethora of work that has claimed that the National Curriculum for Physical Education in England and Wales has not been taught effectively in primary schools (e.g. Evans *et al.* 1996; Gilbert 1998; Harrison 1998; Oxley 1998; Davies 1999; Revell 2000; Speednet Survey 2000; Warburton 2001; Wright 2004). In order to develop subject knowledge and practice, there has been a focus within primary Physical Education around ways of teaching physical skills in order to develop 'the basic building blocks' (Hayden-Davies 2005: 48), but this can be limiting. Sometimes, in our keenness to address the technical needs of our children, the physical aspects of teaching are the main focus. Griggs and McGregor (2012: 230) make an important point here: 'that is not to say that a movement such as a "textbook" forward roll is not a desirable skill to acquire but ideally this would have been selected by the child as one of a dozen different rolls at their disposal, after repeated exploration'.

Meaning-making in primary Physical Education means that the learner gains greater understanding of his or her body through time for play, experimentation and exploration with the use of action, metaphor, analogy, descriptive vocabulary, imagery, pattern, rhythm and pace. Play and exploration are essential to physicality and creativity. Chazen (cited in Wood and Attfield 2002: 198) gives an all-encompassing definition of what play is:

> Playing and growing are synonymous with life itself. Playfulness bespeaks creativity and action, change and possibility of transformation. Play activity thus reflects the very existence of self.

The paradox of play is that play is not, nor should be, easily defined; it can be limitless, complex, sometimes chaotic, non-linear and unpredictable. It can be regarded as trivial and purposeless or deeply serious and purposeful, and is not always content nor context dependent. What is important is that time, space and value is given to play and exploration, as this is the way that children (and adults) try out old and new knowledge, thinking and possibilities individually and with others, as play is a means of creating and preserving friendships.

Exploration and play enables children to discover their bodies (see Figure 1.1). Just watch a baby as he or she responds to the first time he or she grabs hold of a foot and discovers that he or she has toes! Or the first time a young child feels the wind on his or her face or through his or her fingers, especially when he or she moves through a space

■ **Figure 1.1** Exploration of actions and communication of ideas

really fast. The importance of action, exploration and play is recognised in fostering creativity (Piaget 1962; Millar 1967; Vygotsky 1978; Shonkoff and Phillips 2000; Wood and Attfield 2005; Wood 2009). Fisher and Williams (2004) advocate that if play and imagination are encouraged, then teachers and learners are open to new and different approaches. Children build on what they know in order to make meaning, so opportunities for spontaneous exploration and play will enable teachers to see what children know, can do and understand, and how they are applying knowledge and making connections in their learning. Problem-solving, investigative activities and creative improvisation tasks can challenge and enable children to take risks in their learning, try new things and generate new possibilities and knowledge, and during this range of more and less structured activities and opportunities, children will also gain explicit instruction, directed activities, formative feedback and interventions, as appropriate. The Early Years Foundation Stage Curriculum (DCSF 2008) recognises the importance of play and playful approaches, and the example below reinforces the physical potential of this holistic curriculum.

It is easy to dismiss such a child-centred approach, which promotes physical and creative learning, as something that can and does only happen in the Foundation Stage. However, there are a range of supportive arguments for such an approach in Physical Education at Key Stages 1 and 2 with compelling evidence. Since the 1980s (Thorpe *et al.* 1986), the Teaching Games for Understanding (TGfU) approach in Physical Education and community-based sports has gained an ever-increasing following. The approach focuses on problem-solving, and situated and pupil-centred learning, thereby maximising player

---

Scenario

Ben is in reception, and is always moving and physically engaged in play activities. During his role play around a space theme, which takes place in and out of the role-playing area and includes small world play, Ben 'becomes' an astronaut or 'spaceman'. Here, we see he is able to 'read' his physical environment as he puts his 'spaceman' costume on and realises he is bigger now so has to bend and tuck his arms in so that he can get through the door of his pretend rocket. Ben has the motivation and confidence to use his physical capabilities as he demonstrates his awareness and application of faster, bouncy and light movements in his spacesuit, curling movements while getting into the rocket, twisting movements while imagining that the rocket is taking off, pushing and pulling movements around the controls, and slow, heavy, stomping and transfer-of-weight movements once he is 'on the moon'. Once on the moon, Ben lifts heavy moon rock samples (large wooden bricks) and stacks them, and uses the walkie-talkie to report back to base. During this play, he is involved in using and applying locomotor or travelling movements, balancing and object control. He bends, stretches, curls, twists, pushes, pulls, lifts, bounces and steps.

Later, this enabling role-playing experience serves Ben well as he is able to use and apply his knowledge, skills and understanding when his teacher takes the class into the larger space of the hall and asks the children to respond to *Whatever Next*, a book by Jill Murphy. Here, we see the children being engaged by the story narrative and structure as they are encouraged to explore, develop actions, compose and communicate ideas, concepts and emotions.

enjoyment (Butler 2005; Pope 2005; Harvey *et al.* 2010). Light and Fawns (2003: 161) argue that:

> Games taught in physical education using TGfU as a form of educational conversation in which the mind, expressed in speech, and the body, expressed in action, embody the ideal holistic learning experience that simultaneously provides for cognitive, affective, social, and physical learning.

Furthermore, there is much evidence of successful topic-based/thematic-based approaches in gymnastics, dance and outdoor and adventurous activities (QCA Schemes of Work, www.standards.dfes.gov.uk/scheme). Harnessing such opportunities will enable the feeling and seeing of the few boundaries and endless possibilities of what each learner can do with his or her body. Such physical explorations demand the teacher to apply an understanding of pedagogy through a careful balance of unstructured, guided and structured support and challenge in set Physical Education time in school, in cross-curricular connections and in out-of-school opportunities, where appropriate. This will engage the learner in connecting to and building on previous learning and making new physical meanings. Physical education uses the kinaesthetic mode or bodily movement, and provides a vehicle for learners to develop social and cultural awareness such as physical empathy and understanding of difference, as well as feelings, values and ideas. Cognitive development and connection can be seen through the promotion of thinking skills in relation to information processing, reasoning, enquiry, creative and imaginative and evaluation (QCA Schemes of Work, www.standards.dfes.gov.uk/scheme), as well as enhanced memory through physical patterning and repetition, application of and building on previous knowledge (e.g. of tactics and use of weight in problem-solving activities related to games). Greater understanding of other subjects through themes, topics and cross-curricular connections such as dance and maths (e.g. shapes, number, pattern and space or a topic on flight that includes a focus on jumps (elevation) in gymnastics) can also be harnessed. Ensuring relevance in opportunities, activities, themes and ideas that are related to children's interests and that integrate knowledge, skills and understanding will provide greater contexts for meaning.

■ **OPPORTUNITIES** – *Harnessing opportunities within and across the curriculum.* Such opportunities will enable the feeling and seeing of the few boundaries and endless possibilities of what each learner can do with his or her body. Such physical explorations and a careful balance of unstructured, guided and structured support and challenge in set Physical Education time in school, in cross-curricular connections and in out-of-school opportunities will engage the learner in connecting to and building on previous learning and making new physical meanings. Physical Education uses the kinaesthetic mode or bodily movement, and provides a vehicle for learners to develop social and cultural awareness such as physical empathy and understanding of difference, as well as feelings, values and ideas. Cognitive development and connection (Fedewa and Ahn 2011; Rasberry *et al.* 2011) can be seen through enhanced memory through physical patterning and repetition, application of and building on previous knowledge (e.g. of tactics and use of weight in problem-solving activities related to games). Greater understanding of other subjects through themes, topics and cross-curricular connections such as dance and maths (e.g. shapes, number, pattern and space) can also be harnessed.

We understand the challenge of providing a balanced curriculum within Physical Education that enables children to experience different areas of learning such as dance, gymnastics and games, and the specific skill-based elements of teaching within these areas. In order to support such provision, our approach to Physical Education draws on the POWER principles outlined here, and in the early phrases the three movement concepts of *locomotor/travelling*, *balancing/stability* and *object control*. We have taken these three movement concepts in order to share ideas and activities within the specific areas of introducing dance, gymnastics and games that support and challenge children both physically and creatively.

■ **WELL-BEING** – *Developing awareness of health and well-being*
There is pleasure associated with moving, related to physical activity, and sport and regular exercise have beneficial effects such as the development of greater strength, fitness, coordination, stamina and confidence. There is also an increase in endorphins and adrenaline, which can contribute to enhanced self-esteem and other positive psychological states (Flintoff and Scraton 2001, 2005). Further work has raised the status of fun, enjoyment and opportunities for expression within Physical Education (Bond and Stinson 2000/2001, 2007), also related to feelings of happiness and positive identity development. Siddall (2010: 12), in relation to dance, outlines the following benefits:
Physical benefits:

■ Healthier heart and lungs
■ Stronger muscles
■ Stronger bones
■ Better co-ordination, agility and flexibility
■ Improved balance and enhanced spatial awareness
■ Increased physical confidence
■ Improved mental functioning
■ Increased energy expenditure.

Personal and social benefits:

■ Improved general and psychological well-being
■ Greater self-confidence and self-esteem
■ Increased trust
■ Better social skills
■ Reduced isolation and exclusion.

Creative approaches to Physical Education can enable the learner to gain positive experiences from Physical Education, both in and out of school, now and in the future.

■ **ENVIRONMENT** – *Providing a motivating and inclusive climate*
Central to valuing and developing creativity is the idea of 'creativity in relationship' (Chappell *et al.* 2009), where children should be active and motivated learners, and teachers support and challenge based on their pedagogical and subject knowledge. If children are passively receiving information from a teacher, it is difficult to judge whether they are, or are not, motivated or truly engaged. Similarly, if they are required to simply copy the

teacher's movements for the whole session, it is difficult to see whether the children are challenged to build on old, and apply new, knowledge. Although it may seem simple and obvious, Gough (1999) identified three areas that may impact on successful motivation of children, which are worth profiling:

▪ the material or content of the session;
▪ the learner's role within the session; and
▪ the environment in which the learning is taking place.

Creativity is centred around inquisitiveness and a desire to want to know more, to explore and examine, to question and think. Sustaining motivation needs to be carefully thought through as we consider the material or content of the session, the learner's role(s) and the environment. Ideally, we want a motivational climate that fosters children's '*intrinsic motivation*, which refers to doing something because it is inherently interesting or enjoyable, and *extrinsic motivation*, which refers to doing something because it leads to a separable outcome' (Ryan and Deci 2000: 55, original emphasis). Learners need to experience fun out of curiosity, a need to learn new things and develop new skills where the experience becomes a reward in itself. The Physical Education teacher is important here; 'in one sense, intrinsic motivation exists within individuals, in another sense intrinsic motivation exists in the relations between individuals and activities' (Ryan and Deci 2000: 56). Teachers need to be able to be creative and take risks with teaching in the same way we expect learners to be creative risk-takers. This may mean, for example, trying out a range of teaching styles or strategies, providing greater opportunities for ownership from the learners, or exploring different environments for teaching and learning such as *forest school* (Dillon *et al.* 2005). Such opportunities include risk-taking, acceptance of failure, fun, silliness and mess (Chappell *et al.* 2009: 182). According to Jonathan Barnes (2007: 137), creative teachers are simply those who adopt and apply a 'creative state of mind'. The core characteristics that result in creative practice are:

▪ curiosity and questioning;
▪ connection-making;
▪ originality; and
▪ autonomy and ownership.

In these ways, teachers are creative facilitators who are involved in:

▪ encouraging exploration;
▪ nurturing children's insatiable curiosity;
▪ using problem-solving and investigational approaches that stimulate mental activity and self expression, questioning and probing;
▪ providing vivid first-hand experiences in a variety of environments, scaffolding experience for learners;
▪ providing a secure environment where the learner can make private thinking explicit;
▪ communicating effectively;
▪ presenting new ideas as problems to be solved and areas to be investigated, allowing for cognitive restructuring;
▪ promoting positive attitudes;

■   encouraging goal-setting and appropriate task difficulty;
■   providing 'comfortable challenge' (challenge just beyond reach, yet attainable); and
■   building relationships between learner and teacher for 'real' learning, with awareness of individual need.

Furthermore, Grainger *et al.* (2004: 250) argue that just knowing the prescribed curriculum requirements is not enough:

If teachers are to be creative practitioners they need much more than a working knowledge of prescribed curriculum requirements. They need a secure pedagogical understanding and strong subject knowledge, supported by a passionate belief in the potential of creative teaching to engage and inspire hearts and minds. Such teaching depends upon the human interaction.

Everyone can be included in Physical Education so that their experience is an engaging and positive one through the use of appropriate differentiation. It is not appropriate that some learners have felt vulnerable and apprehensive within Physical Education sessions. A commitment to creating a positive, empowering environment is essential. The environments created by us (i.e. as schools and teachers) are key to developing creativity (Wyse and Spendlove 2007). Press and Warburton (2007) are concerned that creativity is a skill that can be practised. Creativity can be pursued as a process and performance. This is a helpful way of thinking as it enables us to develop a creative habit, as at the core is the provision of a teaching environment where creativity can flourish and both the teacher and the children actively engage in the creative process and in the co-construction of creativity.

■   **REVEL** – *Initiating celebration of physical success, achievement and progress.* Learners can progress in and through Physical Education. They should be encouraged to achieve their potential, broaden their horizons and raise their aspirations. Celebrations of physical success, achievement and progress can involve the wider community and media, and may also include partnerships providing enhancement activities. Learners should be involved in evaluating and improving their own performance by engaging in a process of continuity and progression. According to the 2014 Statutory Programmes of Study for Physical Education at Key Stages 1 and 2, at Key Stage 2 children are involved in comparing their performances with previous ones and demonstrate improvement to achieve their personal best. So they need to first describe what they have done, and participate in observing, describing and copying what others have done. They can use what they have learnt to improve the quality and control of their work to identify what makes a performance effective and suggest improvements based on this information. There are many ways to integrate appreciation and achievement into the creative provision of Physical Education.
Through the provision of rich learning experiences, children can progress to become autonomous learners who are *physically literate* (Whitehead 2001; IPLA 2014). It has been suggested by Whitehead (2010: 42) that a physically literate individual:

■   has the motivation to use their physical capacities;
■   can move with poise, economy and confidence in a wide variety of physically challenging situations;

■ is perceptive in 'reading' the physical environment;
■ has a well-established sense of self;
■ has the ability to build relationships with others; and
■ can identify and articulate his or her own movement performance.

More recently Whitehead has described Physical literacy as 'a disposition wherein the individual has the motivation, confidence, physical competence, knowledge and understanding to value and take responsibility for engagement in physical activities for life.' (IPLA 2014)

SUMMARY

Provision for Physical Education that capitalises on children's enthusiasm and motivation to move advocates the creative potential of the body by embracing the POWER principles of a creative approach to Physical Education:

■ **PURPOSE** – *Valuing purposeful physical exploration and meaning-making.*
■ **OPPORTUNITIES** – *Harnessing opportunities within and across the curriculum.*
■ **WELL-BEING** – *Developing awareness of health and well-being.*
■ **ENVIRONMENT** – *Providing a motivating and inclusive climate.*
■ **REVEL** – *Initiating celebration of physical success, achievement and progression.*

Creative teachers value both the physicality of the child and the creativity of the child. This book advocates engagement, motivation and teaching for creativity with the aim of contributing to learners' *physical literacy*.

FURTHER READING

Craft, A. (2000) *Creativity Across the Primary Curriculum*, London: Routledge.
Craft, A. (2001) 'Little c creativity', in A. Craft, B. Jeffrey and M. Leibling (eds), *Creativity in Education*, London: Continuum.
Craft, A. (2002) *Creativity and Early Years Education*, London: Continuum.
Whitehead, M. E. (ed.) (2010) *Physical Literacy Throughout the Lifecourse*, London: Routledge.

CHAPTER 2

PHYSICAL COMPETENCE, PHYSICAL LITERACY AND CREATIVITY

INTRODUCTION

One significant outcome of effective and creative teaching and learning of Physical Education in the primary school is that learners continually enhance their *physical literacy*. In this chapter, we consider first the physical and movement development of young children and the importance of optimum early achievement of physical competence as they progress into the later years in primary school and beyond. This will include key aspects of physical, neuromotor, sensorimotor, movement and language development. We then examine the definition and attributes of the concept of physical literacy and the implications of these for young people as they embark on their lifelong physical literacy journey. Finally, we explore the concept of creativity as an attribute of physical literacy and consider the potential for enhancing creativity when simultaneously developing all other attributes of physical literacy.

KEY ASPECTS

A key element of physical literacy is the development of physical competence. This can be greatly facilitated by enabling children to capitalise on their physical endowment during their early years. Keen (1993: 6) reminds us that 'the human body is built for motion' and is 'designed for efficiency in movement'. Efficiency in movement is dependent upon the optimum integration of muscles and joints. Muscles, which account for 40 per cent of adult mass, provide the means of propulsion, allow us to accelerate and decelerate, and also act as shock absorbers. Keen (1993) goes on to state that for this to be continually managed, a large proportion of the brain is dedicated to achieving gross and fine motor coordination and balance.

Neuromotor development

This can be defined as the relationship between the brain, the nervous system and the muscular system through which movement is facilitated when impulses from nerve fibres pass into muscle fibres. Neuromotor activity is also responsible for the integration of the primitive reflexes that are present at birth and which, if not suppressed in infancy, can lead to motor control problems later in childhood. These include, for example, poor posture in standing and sitting; inability to keep still; poor hand-eye coordination; poor judgement of the speed, power and timing of approaching objects; tracking the path of objects; copying; and poor integration and coordination of the upper and lower sections of the body in movement, as, for example, in swimming (Goddard Blythe 2005: 51). Neuromotor control also involves a series of other systems, including the vestibular, somatosensory and proprioceptive. The vestibular system is responsible for the body's ability to relate to gravity and to manage the speed and direction of movement; the proprioceptive system is influential in control of posture; and the somatosensory system deals with sensation on the skin. Together, these systems provide information to the brain to orchestrate coordination, body awareness and the relationship of one body part to another. The complex interplay of the elements of neuromotor control develops progressively in physically active infants and preschoolers. However, recent research (Goddard Blythe 2012) suggests that many children are seriously delayed in neuromotor development and that this delay interferes with their overall development and their progress in all areas of learning once they start school.

Sensorimotor development

At birth, the brain, which is made up of billions of cells that are not yet connected to each other, is highly active. Cell connections start in the sensorimotor area, at the base of the brain. Feeling and moving are key factors in sensorimotor development, and sensorimotor development underpins all other areas of brain development.

For the essential neural connections to take place in the brain, the cells need to be stimulated. Physical activity is the key stimulus to neural connection. Physical activity is thus the crucial stimulus to brain development in the early years and to brain maintenance throughout life.

Ratey and Hagerman (2008: 4, 245) state that 'exercise cues the building blocks of learning in the brain' and exercise is 'the single most powerful tool to optimise brain function'. They also remind us that 'to keep our brains at peak performance, our bodies need to work hard'. Furthermore, Daniel Wolpert (2012: 35) asserts that although we may claim the function of the brain is to enable us to perceive the world, the reason we have a brain is to produce adaptable and complex movements; 'movement is the only way we have to affect the world around us'. He also reminds us that while sensory, memory and cognitive processes are all important, they are only so because they either drive or suppress future movements.

Cephalo-caudal and proximo-distal development

These two processes dictate the sequence of physical and movement development in infants. Cephalo-caudal development is the 'top-downwards' development, from the head, towards the feet, whereby the upper body increases in strength and control before the lower limbs, with the ankles and feet being the last to mature in this sequence. Evidence for this is the development of locomotion from lying, to sitting, to standing, and finally, when the legs have gained sufficient strength, to walking. Proximo-distal development proceeds from the more central parts of the body outwards. At birth, the central parts of the body are highly active, including the nervous, circulatory, respiratory, digestive and excretory systems. By contrast, there is little evidence of control in the more distal body parts. For example, several years elapse between the apparently indiscriminate flailing of the arms from the shoulders, in early infancy, to the later controlled use of the hands and fingers as in mastering the ability, for example, to prepare text messages at high speed. Successful cephalo-caudal and proximo-distal developments are essential both for complete sensorimotor development and for the achievement of physical competence. Ratey and Hagerman (2008: 3) assert that 'we are born movers', and suggest that we are 'at peril of dulling the brains of the next generation' if we fail to ensure that every young child continually builds on his or her physical competence birthright through frequent physically active play.

Physically active play should include weight-carrying activities such as balancing, running, jumping, rolling, climbing and swinging, which work the large body muscles, help to strengthen the muscular and cardio-respiratory systems, underpin control in fine motor functioning and build an extensive movement vocabulary. Frequent gross motor activity, such as the examples above, is vital for the efficient development of fine motor control. Children who experience difficulty in managing tools, for example, in order to write, may well lack sufficient strength in the wrist and hand. Increasing gross motor activity, especially involving the whole arm from the shoulders, as in climbing, hanging, swinging, swimming, digging or controlling the steering of a balance bike and other wheeled toys, provides additional preparation for supporting the development of fine motor control. As Hoeger and Hoeger (1993: 148) argue, 'movement and physical activity are basic functions for which the human organism was created'. Physical activity is thus paramount for the optimum development of both the brain and the achievement of well-coordinated and controlled movement competence, thereby enabling increasing access for children in relation to all that they do.

Play

In Chapter 1, we drew on Chazen's (cited in Wood and Attfield 2002: 198) all-encompassing definition of play and discussed the importance of *purpose* as *valuing purposeful physical exploration and meaning-making*. We argued that this is a core feature of a creative approach in Physical Education. Here, we continue to develop our argument for *valuing purposeful physical exploration and meaning-making* in relation to play. By the time children start school, they will have experienced more than four years of play; Vygotsky (cited in Singer and Singer 2005) suggests that the act of play extends far beyond the recreational factor, and, indeed, play for children could be seen as the equivalent of work for adults. Play enables children to learn many skills beyond movement competence, such as decision-making, turn-taking, language acquisition and social interaction. The British Heart Foundation (2013) suggests that a rich play experience should include four types of play, namely: 'unstructured' or 'free' play, 'child-initiated' play, 'focused learning' play, and play involving 'highly structured physical activities'. Free play is defined by Adrian Voce (2006: 2) as 'freely chosen, personally directed, intrinsically motivated behaviour and without adult intervention'. In child-initiated play, significant others such as playmates, peers, older children, parents and other adults can extend children's learning by adding stimulus, and offering support, encouragement, feedback and modelling, and can contribute richness to the development of children's communication skills. Focused learning play is initiated by an adult, with the child then taking over while the adult prompts, gives feedback, guides and facilitates the child's discovery. Play involving highly structured physical activities in more formal settings is pre-planned with learning outcomes designed to engage with children's needs. Ideally, this should further facilitate the provision of breadth, variety and richness within children's play experiences, increasing movement vocabulary and language mastery.

Singer and Singer (2005) suggest that play provides for creativity and spontaneity, poses problem-solving opportunities and promotes intellectual growth. However, free play as the sole play opportunity, without any adult interaction, is not sufficient. Children are normally naturally active, energetic and inquisitive, physically competent, wide-ranging and self-challenging in their play and greatly benefit from teacher observation, support and challenge, as appropriate. The limitations of free play can leave children constrained within the boundaries of their own experience and by the absence of further stimulus to develop their creative play. A sufficient play experience is best achieved through a mixture of unstructured play, child-initiated play, focused learning and through the incorporation of structured physical activities both in preschool and in school settings.

Scenario

Jack started his experience on wheels with a tricycle at the age of 2, such that, when offered a 'balance bike', he was initially not very impressed! Pedalling to go along on a stable vehicle was fine but balancing on an unstable one was not! He found it a challenge to establish and maintain postural control in order to keep the bike upright while getting onto it and holding a sitting position. However, a few weeks later, after repeated trials and the encouragement of his enthusiastic parents, he found that he could balance, holding the handlebars and sitting on the saddle with his feet on the floor. Jack was not one to give up on a new toy, so it was not long before he started to walk along on the bike. Once outdoors, walking led to striding. Striding led to taking his feet off the ground momentarily and putting them back down to stop, in order to straighten the bike up again or to turn around. Jack is now a great balance bike rider, able to get on, start, walk, run, lift his feet off the ground, glide along, and put his feet back down to stop with control. Now, at the age of 3, he also creates his own journeys along the paths in the local park and chats about what he is doing.

What can we observe and surmise about Jack's physical competence by comparing the two photographs (Figures 2.1 and 2.2)? He has developed in terms of postural control, locomotion, and static and dynamic balance; he has probably had lots of exercise; he has gained knowledge of how to handle the bike; and he seems to have the motivation and determination to persist with the challenge and looks as if he is confident and enjoying himself. What might we expect Jack to be able to do in the future? Having established the fundamental movement capacity of 'balance', he might go on to develop other specialised cycling skills or to look for other opportunities to discover how well he can balance. However, Jack's early cycling opportunities are not those that are experienced by all twenty-first-century children.

■ **Figure 2.1** Striding Jack

■ **Figure 2.2** Riding Jack

Delayed Movement Development and Developmental Coordination Disorder (DCD)

The term 'container generation' has been used when referring to infants who were too often carried around or constrained in seats, rockers and beanbags and thereby deprived of as much tummy time and free play exploration time as they needed. Concerns have also been expressed about 'couch potato' children whose lifestyles are more sedentary than they ought to be. Such concerns about inactive young children have led the British Heart Foundation (2012, www.bhf.org.uk) to publish Physical Activity Guidelines. Relating to inactivity, Goddard Blythe (2012) concludes, in the results of her recent research, that a significant percentage of children are starting school with immature motor skills and with postural instability. This may be due to inactive lifestyles, which have led to neuromotor immaturity and to the continued presence of residual reflexes that ought to have been suppressed by the age of 3. She notes that there is a direct correlation between immature motor skills and educational achievement, and states that neuromotor immaturity is a barrier to learning. For example, if children need to give conscious attention to their standing and sitting posture and to trying to control involuntary disturbances in their movement, the demands placed on their ability to concentrate on their learning in class is seriously disrupted. Young children who are seen to be fidgeting and are asked to sit still may need to give all their attention just to the task of sitting still, such that if they also try to give attention to the learning activity, they are unable to do both. Similarly, children who are seen to slide down in their chairs so that it is difficult to undertake tabletop tasks are sometimes thought to be trying to avoid the task, whereas they may actually be lacking the postural control and core stability to sustain upright posture. With reference to infant reflexes, children who have retained the tonic neck reflex may be seen to look away from the paper when trying to write or to lose control of the pencil on the paper when trying also to look at the paper (Cheatum 2000).

DCD is characterised by difficulty in planning and executing smooth, coordinated movements; however, we must be mindful of age/stage appropriateness in development here. It has been reported (NHS n.d.) that as many as one child in 12 may be affected by DCD. This condition can have a profound effect on children's ability to participate in many aspects of Physical Education, especially manipulative activities such as games when they have to select and apply specific movements in a group or team setting, in a constantly changing environment. Competitive activity requiring quick decision-making, with no time to plan the required movement response, may prove to be an impossible challenge. However, when provided with appropriate resources, and opportunities to explore and progressively acquire single skills, without peer pressure, children with DCD can be successful and enjoy a rewarding experience. Children with DCD can amass a wide movement vocabulary alongside their peers and can develop movement memory and movement quality. Fortunately, educators are increasingly aware and alert to deficits such as these, and some school settings have established forms of screening for children in fundamental motor skills, balance and postural control, with support sessions and increased gross motor activity, to enable them to catch up at the earliest opportunity. In her longitudinal study of 15,000 children born in 2000 and 2001, with results published in 2010, Goodard Blythe (2012) found that children who failed at nine months to reach four key gross motor development milestones of sitting, crawling, standing and practising taking first steps were found to be behind in ability tests at 5 years of age. She also found that delay in gross and fine motor development in a child's first year was significantly associated with cognitive development and behavioural adjustment at age 5. Furthermore, Campbell (2013) reported that thousands of children aged 11 years are starting secondary school not able to throw a ball, catch, jump or run. Creative teaching of movement vocabulary in the Early Years and Key Stages 1 and 2 can ensure that the next generation does not suffer this deficit.

Movement vocabulary is to movement as the dictionary is to the spoken vocabulary of words. There are millions of movements that are capable of human performance, and it is the responsibility of all movement facilitators to enable young children continually to increase their repertoire of movements, in building both a rich movement vocabulary and a rich vocabulary of spoken words with which to communicate about movement. Exploring and developing movement patterns can form the focus of teaching and learning in the Early Years and in Key Stage 1. Table 2.1 includes a series of fundamental movement categories, namely balance, locomotion, flight, manipulation, projection, construction and non-verbal communication. By allocating individual movements to named categories, it is possible to cluster related movements.

Language and movement

Young children bring to their movement and language learning extensive tacit knowledge. Tacit knowledge (or habitual movement) is that which is employed as we move, but that which we cannot readily verbalise, because it is pre-reflective; an adult example is that of driving a car. Much of the ability to achieve both the massive range of movements and the fast-paced decisions required to control the vehicle, negotiate other traffic and obey the rules of the road is internalised rather than explicit. Nevertheless, for young children, the significance of language acquisition through moving cannot be underestimated. We therefore turn our attention now to the development of language through movement and the development of movement through language. Kiphard (1995) reminds us that 'movement is a child's first language', and 'movement is the first medium of expression of the physical and emotional condition of an individual'. Asher (1983: 3) states that 'children decode language through the intimate integration and subsequent relationship of language and bodily movement'. Earliest forms of communication are non-verbal and are also highly significant in facilitating the conveying of messages from the infant to the carer(s), and vice versa. Bee (2010: 205) suggests that in the *prelinguistic phase*, 'babies successfully use gestures and body language in consistent ways to communicate meaning'. Evidence includes facial communication, as in smiling, pointing and waving to say goodbye. This early use of gestures, often acquired from copying those used by carers, introduces the skills of observing and translating observation into bodily actions. These important skills can then be extended and developed by teachers within the Physical Education curriculum.

Enabling language learning through movement

MacIntyre (2000: 8) argues that 'the spoken word includes body language which enables it to be readily assimilated'. Body language remains an influential factor in learning language through movement, so in acquiring language, young children readily relate to

▨ **Table 2.1** Some movement categories, with examples

Balance *– vocabulary to enhance stable support and postural control*

on front	on back	on side	on seat	on hands and feet	on hands and knees
on knees	on feet	on one hand and one foot	on one foot	sliding	upside down, as in handstand
on elevated, wide and narrow surface	rocking	scooting	biking	floating	

Locomotion *– vocabulary to enhance travel from place to place*

creeping	slithering	crawling	stepping	walking	gliding
trotting	jogging	running	dodging	pouncing	rolling
hopping along	skipping	galloping	bunny jumping along	cartwheeling	
pulling	pushing	swinging	climbing	wading	swimming

Flight *– vocabulary to enhance projecting oneself off the ground and back down to land*

landing on two feet	taking off	jumping up	jumping along	jumping onto two feet	
jumping around	jumping off	jumping over	jumping with turn	taking off on one foot	
landing on one foot	hopping	hopscotch	leaping	assisted flight	abseiling

---

Manipulation

holding	feeling	grasping	gripping	drawing	tracing
guiding	cutting	pegging	threading	pulling	shoving
releasing	moulding	picking up	putting down	typing	
receiving a rolled object	receiving a thrown object	computer-mouse management			

Projection

placing	rolling	bouncing	throwing	striking	heading
aiming	kicking	punting	volleying	flicking	flinging
spinning	skimming	serving	driving	putting	goal shooting

Construction

grasping	picking up	lifting	carrying	arranging	assembling
adjusting	stacking	building	dismantling	storing	

Communication (non-verbal)

pointing	waving	clapping	smiling	frowning	leaning
bowing	curtsying	turning towards	turning away		

the vocabulary used by their carers and the language system that they are exposed to on a daily basis. Typically, this is vocabulary associated with movement, including:

■ nouns, especially those used to name parts of the body, such as hands, feet, elbows, knees; familiar locations, such as chair, floor, step; and manipulative resources, such as ball, bat, bike;
■ verbs, such as lie, sit, stand, clap, point;
■ adverbs, such as quickly, slowly, steadily;
■ spatial vocabulary, such as up, down, behind, over, under; and
■ short phrases, such as 'clap hands', 'lie down', 'roll ball'.

Dean and Goss (cited in Guildenhuys 1996: 14) claim that 'movement-based learning has the capacity to generate empowering environments for the learning of language'. Similarly, Bruner (1983: 23) states that 'movement based interactions provide an environment in which the learner is immersed in understandable messages, where language can be placed in context naturally and meaningfully'. This is further supported by Hopper *et al.* (2000: 91), where they suggest that 'translating movements into spoken language in a variety of contexts offers a treasure chest of descriptive, directional and action words for children to explore, experience and use'.

Enabling movement learning through language

Movement learning through language has the potential for ready assimilation, as Asher (1983: 4) supports: 'language is orchestrated to the choreography of the human body'. However, it is important to note that learning movement through language depends on the quality of the language used. McIntyre (2010: 14), in discussing the *principles of lucidity*, suggests that lucid speaking is highly explicit, using:

> the same word or phrase for the same things . . . and different words or phrases for different things . . . Lucidity enables context to be built before new points are introduced . . . Lucidity accelerates perceptual processing, pruning the enormous combinatorial tree of possible internal models in the listener's brain as quickly as possible, ahead of conscious thought.

This is of paramount importance in providing verbal explanations of movement, in order to minimise intervention in the movement experience by maximising speed of comprehension of the intended movement response. For example, choice of accurate vocabulary speeds up processing response time, as it precludes the need to translate the spoken word before applying it to movement. A common example of this is asking children to 'point their toes', when the intended movement outcome is to 'extend the ankles', since it is the muscles around the ankle that are required to initiate and perform the movement, and, therefore, the neural messages need to go to the receptors in the ankle, rather than to those in the toes. In a different example, confusion in movement response can arise where a non-specific term is used, such as 'roly-poly' or 'somersault', when tasking children to roll, rather than employing the technical vocabulary for rolling, such as roll sideways, roll forwards or roll backwards. Here, the principle of *lucidity* should be applied, so that learners can interpret specific tasks by applying known technical terms to named activities.

Robert Stenwell (cited in Gladwell 2008) refers to *practical intelligence* in effective communication, which he suggests includes knowing what to say to whom and knowing how to say it for maximum effect. In movement learning, the choice of vocabulary and content of the language used in a task setting should be both succinct and positive. For example, if the intended movement response to an instruction is not to run, it is preferable to say 'walk', since to say 'don't run' almost inevitably results in running, as the last word heard was 'run'.

The integration of language and movement, whether through learning to move or moving to learn, is a rich source of successful movement and cognitive development in young children, and is a key fundamental contributor to physical literacy.

During the previous chapter, we suggested that rich learning experiences can enable learners to become increasingly physically literate (Whitehead 2010: 11–12). It is worth referring to the current definition of physical literacy:

> Physical Literacy can be described as a disposition wherein the individual has the motivation, confidence, physical competence, knowledge and understanding to value and take responsibility for engagement in physical activities for life.
>
> (2014 IPLA)

Physical literacy should not be viewed as an end product to be aspired to, but rather a state in which we live throughout our lives. We are all, to a greater or lesser extent, physically literate and our physical literacy is influenced by our endowment at birth, our early upbringing opportunities and our subsequent lifestyle choices. Each child is continually travelling along his or her own physical literacy journey. It is therefore all the more important that children's physical literacy is nurtured from their earliest days, enabling them to capitalise on and enhance, rather than suppress, their movement competence, confidence and motivation, and enable them to increase their knowledge and understanding of movement and develop their commitment to ongoing physical activity. We argue that one of the key aspects to optimum physical literacy is the attainment of optimum physical competence. To achieve maximum physical competence, infants and young children should engage in physically active play for the greater part of the waking day, in short bouts, with appropriate rests, playing alone, alongside other children, and with the supportive and developmental participation of family members and carers. Both the neuromotor and sensorimotor systems develop exponentially as a result of maximising active play, of limiting sedentary activity to just that which is essential for healthy growth and through the promotion of frequent active play throughout childhood.

Motivation to be physically active determines, to a large extent, the possibility of achieving optimum physical competence. Most infants strive to move in order to explore the world around them through trial and error, determination and drive to reach new goals, practice and repetition, and these are all evidence of the motivation to succeed and to discovering that success breeds success. All the more detrimental, then, is a situation in which a child loses motivation and shies away from physical activity. This may be due to loss of confidence, feelings of poor self-image, seeming lack of success, loss of enjoyment and satisfaction, and feelings of inability to achieve. It is worth exploring how such negative situations could occur, if a loving, positive, supportive and stimulating environment surrounds the child.

In discussion with trainee primary school teachers about their motivation and loss of motivation to participate in Physical Education during their own primary school years, they cited positive experiences that influenced their motivation as:

'It was great to be out of the classroom, getting good exercise'
'I had knowledgeable teachers'
'We got positive and supportive feedback'
'The teacher showed respect for us all'
'I was not good at PE, but the teacher encouraged me and gave me confidence'
'I was best at PE, so always had a very good report'
'Learning in PE was fun'
'We tried a variety of activities and discovered what we could do'

Negative experiences cited were almost exclusively not about the subject matter of Physical Education, nor about becoming physically educated or physically literate, but related to issues around organisation, management and administration, such as:

'the crowded and impersonal routine for changing clothes'
'getting cold outdoors'
'having to work in bare feet on dirty floors'
'standing around with nothing to do'
'being picked last for teams'
'being watched doing things badly'

Negative issues such as these can be addressed and overcome at the school planning stage and through effective initial and continuing professional development. Fostering a 'can-do' attitude, valuing effort as well as achievement, and providing access to positive outcomes can go a long way to helping all to maintain a desire and determination to participate in physical activity and build an active lifestyle.

The broader definition of physical literacy cites a number of attributes that are specifically relevant to primary school children, enabling them to contribute to the quality of their lives.

First, that physical competence enables the learner to move with poise, economy of effort, sensitivity and fluent self-expression through non-verbal communication. Second, that as children gain physical competence, they concurrently enhance knowledge and understanding of their movement, gaining the freedom to explore more widely, and to use their intelligence, imagination and ingenuity as creative learners. Third, that 'articulate interaction with the environment' (Whitehead 2010: 13) is enhanced, as the physically competent children are able to 'read' the environment and anticipate movement needs, thereby enabling them to transfer movement knowledge from one situation to another.

Let us take a moment to make connections here to the POWER principles that were introduced in Chapter 1. Throughout childhood, provision of *purpose* and *opportunities* are key in developing awareness of *well-being* in the promotion of physical competence and physical literacy. Through indoor and outdoor *environments*, enriched with appropriate resources, natural, manufactured and with play partners, both adults and children, learners can *revel* in celebration of physical success, achievement and progression. In early childhood, clear indoor spaces in the home enable children to move independently and safely in their explorations and to move with greater finesse and control as they mature. Maximising opportunities for active play in the home, even where space is limited, including, for example, through rhythmic activities such as exercise to music and Wii play, can add to overall levels of physical activity and help to counter the 'couch potato' syndrome of inactivity. Perry (2001: 118) suggests that 'outdoor play settings may be the one place where children can independently orchestrate their own negotiations with the physical and social environment and gain the clarity of selfhood necessary to navigate later in life'. The variety of outdoor environments may include gardens, parks, streets, playgrounds, woods, fields, shallow pools, sea, snow, trees, grass, sand, beaches and icy puddles. Here, children can be engaged meaningfully, purposefully and with imagination. More consideration is made to creative spaces in Chapter 9. If we add to these the benefits to be gained in terms of developing their physical literacy through enhancing confidence, motivation, imagination, knowledge, understanding and communication, we have overwhelming evidence for the benefits of outdoor play. Thus, for children in school, not only is playtime important for their development through free play, but the inclusion of outdoor as well as indoor learning in Physical Education is essential in promoting optimum physical literacy.

In the scenario below, we follow Emma on her physical literacy journey, from her early cycling experience along the smooth, hard surface of the driveway at home, to experiences in a wide range of environments, on a variety of bikes, both alone and with many significant others, including both children and adults. As with Jack on page 16, the initial focus is on the movement capability of balance, as this is such a crucial fundamental movement acquisition for all children. In this scenario, however, we see how Emma progresses from her early acquisition of balance and general movement learning

---

Scenario

Emma was just 2 years old when she set off along the driveway in her garden, enjoying her first experience of walking along while sitting on her balance bike. By the age of 3, she was a competent balance bike rider, along the drive and across the lawn in her garden and with a parent in the local park. She used her avid imagination to create stories that were played out as journeys, travelling to visit toys distributed around the garden and she found out what happens when you go too fast or try to ride into the sand pit! Once she transferred from a balance bike to a bike with pedals, she soon became a fully confident and competent bike rider and was ready to venture onto the local cycle paths with her parents. She progressed from there to following a parent along the cycle ways in local roads. She gained her cycling proficiency award and at about the same time, the garden was converted into a self-created BMX-type track, with humps and hollows, sharp turns and mud, for making up and practising tricks, devising competitions and designing races with friends. Emma became an avid, intelligent, creative and independent bike rider who cycled with confidence and with the quality and efficiency of movement that made bike riding look easy. She also cycled daily to and from school and wherever she needed to go in the local community. By the time she left her primary school, Emma was a member of the local BMX club, went on cycling holidays with her family and knew a great deal not only about how to cycle, but also about cycling sports. She was also keen to try out extreme sports such as freestyle motocross.

into movement mastery and overall physical literacy. She takes full advantage of her high level of movement competence and branches out to expand her experience into sophisticated pursuits, resulting in enjoyment, as well as social development and overall maturity.

From this scenario, we see that factors such as the variety of environments experienced, the quality of movement achieved, the transfer of motor skills and knowledge from one situation to another, and the application of intelligent behaviour all contribute to the enhancement of her physical literacy in terms of physical competence, knowledge and understanding of movement, motivation, confidence, imagination, self-esteem, communication and health promoting activity.

Creativity and physical literacy

In this, the final section of this chapter, we explore the concept of creativity as an attribute of physical literacy. Consideration is given both to the potential for enhancing creativity when simultaneously developing all other attributes of physical literacy, and to the advantages of exploring creativity in movement learning as a further means of developing physical literacy.

To take ownership of becoming an imaginative and creative mover requires the learner to 'move outside the box' and to be prepared to rediscover the quality of exploration in movement that was so prominent in infancy. To have the confidence and motivation to adopt a discovery-learning approach, to be prepared to engage in 'trial and error', to have a willingness to embark on a movement path and experience that is flexible and be open to change as it progresses may be new challenges for the learner. Having a new idea and then drawing on the existing bank of movement experience to work with that idea, to bring it to fruition, calls for considerable imagination and tenacity and an ability to suspend disbelief. Taking the example of Makonde carvers of southern Tanzania who work with the mpingo wood, the carver has an idea and vision of what may emerge from the wood as a finished product, but in the process employs the skills learnt since childhood and years of experience to reveal a completely original and personal product.

In Figure 2.3, the key attributes of physical literacy are collated under the three headings of *Movement Attributes*, *Affective Attributes* and *Interactive Attributes*. Set alongside these are charted some ways in which creativity enhances physical literacy and some suggestions as to how creativity can be promoted by developing all aspects of physical literacy. Taking an example from the box entitled *Affective Attributes*, learners whose confidence is strong as a result of having achieved skilful performance levels and an extensive movement vocabulary, along with sound knowledge and understanding of movement, are well prepared to 'move outside the box' of prior experience in order to explore new and creative movement territory. Taking an example from the section *Contributions of creativity to enhancing physical literacy*, creative learners can draw on their knowledge and motivation to increase their movement vocabulary and appreciation of alternative movement responses to tasks. In this way, confidence may also grow.

SUMMARY

Developing the imaginative and creative attribute of a physically literate individual is greatly enhanced by having already made progress and by continuing to make progress in all other attributes. However, exploration of creativity in movement also contributes to achieving

Contributions of Creativity to Enhancing Physical Literacy	Attributes of Physical Literacy	Contributions of Physical Literacy to Enhancing Creativity
⇒	⇐ ⇒	⇐
	Movement Attributes	
Through tackling self-set as well as teacher-promoted creative challenges, learners can explore alternative aspects of movement vocabulary, enhance and evaluate creative experiences and thereby also gain further knowledge and understanding of physical competence	Physical Competence Knowledge Understanding	Increasing movement vocabulary and enhancing skilful performance can expand potential for creative activity Through movement observation, analysis of self and others and through the study of movement, learners can bring greater knowledge to their creative endeavours
	Affective Attributes	
Enabling creative learners to enhance their confidence, motivation and self-esteem through encouraging and supporting their playfulness, inquisitiveness, creative enquiry, experimentation, searching, failing and succeeding, provides increased depth to physical literacy	Confidence Motivation Self-esteem	Building increasing confidence engendered through skilful performance and familiarity with wide applications of movement, enhances intrinsic motivation and self-esteem generated through achievement and success
	Interactive Attributes	
Creative exploration of movement spaces, the texture of the environment, work surfaces and access to various levels, pathways, and directions of movement, enhances learners' physical literacy	Environments – indoor and outdoor	Skilful exploration of a wide range of environments enables learners to apply related experience from one environment to another, thereby extending opportunities for the flowering of creativity
Working creatively alongside younger learners and peers as well as with older children and adults strengthens the ability to engage in social aspects of physical literacy, such as cooperation and competition	People	Interacting comfortably in movement with younger learners and peers as well as with older children and adults can stimulate and strengthen the creative the experience
Free, creative movement exploration of natural resources, man-made and manufactured equipment promotes extensive variety, proficiency and enrichment in the experience and management of resources and equipment	Resources	Having the ability to interact with a wide range of natural, man-made and manufactured resources, increases exploratory and creative opportunities

▨ **Figure 2.3** Relationships between physical literacy and creativity greater potential in physical literacy. In this chapter, we have considered children's physical and movement development in the context of becoming physically competent, laying down the foundations in the early years and then building on and consolidating these throughout the primary school years. Through applying an understanding of the processes of early childhood physical and movement competence development and of factors that enable children to embark upon their physical literacy journey, we can help to ensure that the curriculum content offered is appropriate and that teaching chimes with children's learning needs. We then examined the concept of physical literacy as a lifelong entitlement, extending beyond becoming physically educated. Finally, we explored the concept of creativity as an enriching feature in developing physical literacy. In conclusion, creative teachers can help children to capitalise on their innate and unique movement potential, educate learners in developing their physical competence, and inspire learners to increase their knowledge and understanding. Creative teachers can also set role models to assist learners in maintaining their own motivation, goal-setting, challenge and achievement, build self-esteem and self-confidence in their learners, and reinforce the attributes of physical literacy in enhancing quality of life.

FURTHER READING

Goddard-Blythe, S. (2005) *The Well Balanced Child*, Stroud: Hawthorne Press.
Maude, P. (2001) *Physical Children, Active Teaching*, Buckingham: Open University Press.
Whitehead, M. E. (ed.) (2010) *Physical Literacy Throughout the Lifecourse*, London: Routledge.

CHAPTER 3

INTRODUCING DANCE ACTIVITIES

INTRODUCTION

This chapter offers ways of introducing dance activities to children in the Foundation Stage and at Key Stage 1. The next chapter, 'Developing dance', focuses on opportunities that are suggested as being more suited to children at Key Stage 2. In both dance chapters, we argue that dance is an art form that cultivates the physical, creative, cognitive, emotional, social and artistic development of children. It has been argued that dance is natural and compelling as children can express themselves naturally through movement (Giguere 2006), and in this way, movement can be considered as the first language. Young children move and respond within the context of the moment, as Lee (2008: 79) reminds us that 'it is through our bodies that we encounter and experience the world and through our bodies we communicate responses to it'. Movement and dance activities can build on and be developed from physical and social play activities as Susan Isaacs (1954: 32) stated that 'play is the child's means of living and of understanding life', and children try out physical activities for enjoyment, to test limitations, develop mastery, and naturally and sponta-neously challenge themselves physically through play (Davies 2003). During such play experiences, which can occur in indoor and outdoor environments, children will also have engaged with basic movement skills such as locomotion/travelling, balance/stability and the manipulation and control of props and objects in their play, as examined in Chapter 2.

Furthermore, 'when children have the opportunity to physically play or dance freely in a safe, encouraging environment, they connect new ideas to personal experiences . . . they notice that their individual movements have value and that experiences build upon earlier established ones to develop new skills. Perhaps most important, they learn they can have fun experiencing the joy of movement' (Jiesamfoek 2012: 204).

Dance, as many other physical activities, can enhance physical development through the use of the whole body and body parts, motion, coordination, strength, kinaesthetic memory and endurance. However, there are also many creative and artistic benefits of dance for young children. Penny Greenland (1995: 1) has stated that creative movement 'includes, enables, embraces', and dance activities offer opportunities for the physical expression of emotions and social awareness through encounters, interactions and cooperation. Creative dance has also been found to develop children cognitively through enhanced concentration and focus (Stinson 1998), and greater attention, speed, retention, application of thinking skills and enjoyment of learning (Sacha and Ross 2006). Furthermore, Karen Bond (2001: 42), in particular, has noted that a child's dance experience involves artistic practice, including sensory awareness, spatial focus, personal stylistic preferences, imagination, intellectual engagement, commitment to practice and performance, self-discipline, and form-making abilities. In addition, Bond and Stinson (2000/2001) suggest that children have 'superordinary' experiences in dance, which include bodily resonance, excitement, relaxation, freedom, sense of inner or true self, and loss of awareness of the outside world.

Introducing dance activities involves building on children's physical play experiences where children will have engaged with rich sensory experiences and learned about themselves through exploration of coordination, speed and kinaesthetic response. Providing a motivating environment that values the 'joy of movement' where young learners are encouraged to explore and try out movement with their bodies is important, as Lindqvist (2001) found in her study of the relationships between play and dance with 6–8 year olds. Lindqvist (2001: 41) argues that young children were motivated by purposeful physical exploration and creative meaning making as they engaged with themes to stimulate their dance and movement activities. Here, they were creating their own narratives in their movement play and 'characterizing figures, roles and actions'. This harnessed the potential of movement and dance opportunities in a holistic way, within and across the curriculum.

In this chapter, we will explore a range of suggested themes and stimuli as ways of introducing creative dance to young learners, which will include opportunities within and across the curriculum. There will also be ways of developing physical aspects of locomotion, body balance and object control through dance. Use of narrative and imagery to enhance creative movement composition will be explored, and Rudolph Laban's (1948, 1966, 1984) categories of movement as body awareness and actions, spatial awareness, effort/dynamics/qualities and relationships will be introduced. Furthermore, ways of planning and assessing will be examined.

KEY ASPECTS

 Young learners can be supported and challenged to create movement when presented with different stimuli; a stimulus is something that inspires and provides a starting point for the exploration of movement ideas. Stimuli can be grouped in ways that link to the senses:

- **Visual** (what you see) – pictures, photographs, paintings, DVD excerpts, colours, shapes.
- **Auditory** (what you hear) – music, sound effects, percussion, rhythms, rhymes, repetitive phrases, poetry.
- **Kinaesthetic** (what you do and/or what you feel – emotion) – actions, movements phrases, sequences.
- **Tactile** (what you touch) – materials, fabrics, props, objects.
- **Ideational** (from the brain) – ideas or problems that need to be solved with a movement response – 'What would happen if I tried a high movement, a low movement and a fast movement?'

Some stimuli cross a number of types, such as children's picture books, which are potentially visual, auditory, tactile and kinaesthetic.

Using stimuli for movement and dance can be integrated as part of the holistic Early Years Foundation Stage (2008), where young learners are engaged in playful and creative opportunities within all areas of development: physical development, creative development, personal, social and emotional, communication, language and literacy, mathematical development, and knowledge and understanding of the world. Table 3.1 shows how movement and dance activities can be connected to these areas.

Using different stimuli as starting points for creative dance can be used within the Foundation Stage, but stimuli can also be used for dance in the National Curriculum at Key Stage 1. Cross-curricular opportunities can also be used to best effect at Key Stage 1. At Key Stage 1, learners will be engaged in responding imaginatively to different stimuli, expressing and communicating ideas and feelings, as well as drawing on the basic skills of, for example, travelling, being still, making a shape, jumping, turning and gesturing. They will also be able to change the rhythm, speed, level and direction of their movements, and create and perform dances using simple movement patterns, including those from different times and cultures. During Key Stage 1, learners will acquire and develop dance skills through experimenting with a wide range of actions, with basic dance structure and composition. As the repertoire of movement grows, learners will be able to select and apply movements and simple compositional devices to create their own dances. When watching their own and others' work, learners will develop appreciation of movement quality and effort (adapted from the previous and current National Curriculum, www.dcfs.gov.uk). Within this, a focus on the three areas of locomotion, balance/stability and object control can be helpful. There are a variety of themes that are suitable for introducing and developing dance activities that can incorporate a range of stimuli.

Themes and starting points that work well for children aged 4–7 years are, for example:

■ action songs and rhymes;
■ all about me;
■ toys, props and objects;
■ bears;
■ times of the day; and
■ weather.

Here are some brief starting points for use of the themes for introducing dance.

Action songs and rhymes

Often, very young children's early experiences and starting points for introducing movement and dance activities are action songs and rhymes. Table 3.2 shows a list of first lines and types of songs and rhymes adapted from www.bookstart.org.uk. Rhymes from other countries (in English and/or other languages) can be found at www.mamalisa.com/world.

Here, young learners can engage physically, cognitively and socially with rhythms, rhymes and repetition as they listen, copy actions and respond to the songs and rhymes. The structure of the songs and rhymes can develop confidence, coordination, control, concentration and movement memory. Initial work may involve the practitioner leading

■ **Table 3.1** Movement and dance and connections to learning in Early Years Foundation Stage

Physical Development	Moving safely, imaginatively and with confidence (*locomotion*) Experiencing a range of gross motor movements and fine motor movements (*locomotion/body balance*) The development of spatial awareness (*locomotion/body balance*) Moving with bodily control, coordination, flexibility and balance (*body balance*) Dancing with props, developing manipulative skills (*object control*) Keeping healthy – dance as part of a healthy lifestyle
Creative Development	Communicating ideas, thoughts and feelings non-verbally through movement Using the imagination to create ideas, characters and narratives Making movement responses
Personal, Social and Emotional Development	Having an enjoyable, exciting and motivating time Working individually, with a partner and as part of a group Developing trust and cooperation Selecting and using movement ideas independently and with others Exploring feelings and views of self and others – including other cultures and beliefs Accepting the moral code on which discipline and courtesy within the group is based Interacting with a group
Communication, Language and Literacy Development	The use of sounds, music, words, poems, rhymes, texts and stories as stimuli for and accompaniment to dance The use of language to imagine and recreate roles and ideas in the dance Interaction – negotiating plans and activities and developing conversational skills Appreciation – talking about personal dance performance Observation – talking about the dance performance of others Developing a vocabulary of movement
Mathematical Development	Developing spatial awareness Use of numbers and counting Making shapes Exploring size Exploring direction Developing pattern and sequencing
Knowledge and Understanding of the World	Making recordings of observations and through drawings, photographs and using equipment such as video cameras Developing curiosity and asking questions about why things happen and how things work Observing, ordering and sequencing events

Fingerplay songs that can include whole body movement	*This Little Piggy* *Round and Round the Garden* *10 Fat Sausages* *1-2-3-4-5 Once I Caught a Fish Alive* *Five Little Men in a Flying Saucer* *Cows in the Kitchen* *Incey Wincey Spider* *Hickory Dickory Dock* *Twinkle Twinkle*
Movements songs (action/ bouncing/dancing)	*Down in the Bottom of the Deep Blue Sea* *Five Little Ducks* *Five Little Monkeys* *Dingle Dangle Scarecrow* *Down in the Jungle* *Heads Shoulders Knees and Toes* *Here We Go Looby Loo* *Here We Go Round the Mulberry Bush* *Hey Diddle Diddle* *Hickory Dickory Dock* *Hokey Cokey* *Horsey Horsey* *Humpty Dumpty* *If You're Happy and You Know It* *I'm a Little Teapot* *Ride a Cock Horse* *Ring a Ring a Roses* *Row Row Row Your Boat* *Skip to My Loo* *The Bear Went Over the Mountain* *The Big Ship Sails* *The Grand Old Duke of York* *The Wheels on the Bus* *This is the Way the Ladies Ride* *We All Clap Hands Together* *What Shall We Do With a Lazy Baby* *Wind the Bobbin Up* *Little Peter Rabbit* *Open Shut Them* *Pat a Cake* *Pickles in the Pickle Pot* *Roly Poly Roly Poly Up Up Up* *Teddy Bear Teddy Bear* *Jack Be Nimble* *Jelly on a Plate*
Number songs that need actions and movements	*1-2-3-4-5 Once I Caught a Fish Alive* *Two Little Dickie Birds* *10 Fat Sausages* *Five Little Men in a Flying Saucer* *Five Little Ducks* *Five Currant Buns in a Baker's Shop* *Five Little Monkeys* *Five Little Speckled Frogs* *I Have 10 Little Fingers*

and sharing action vocabulary, but soon both children and adults can also begin to explore, create and develop their own songs, rhymes, actions and movements. For example, movement ideas for *Incey Wincey Spider* may include crawling, creeping and climbing spiders that tumble and fall. For *Hickory Dickory Dock*, there may be scurrying mice moving up and down the clock, short, sharp changes of direction, and jerking, rhythmic clockwork actions.

All about me

This theme can enhance awareness of *locomotion* and *balance and stability* by using large body parts, small body parts, basic movement skills, recognition of changes to the body when active, coordination and control, such as starting and stopping, and use of body in space. The theme can develop from action songs and rhymes such as *Heads, Shoulders, Knees and Toes* or *Hokey Cokey*. Table 3.3 shows what an exploration of the range and potential of different body parts could include.

Challenges could be set, such as: 'Can you shake your hands to the ceiling and then bend over and touch your toes?' 'How many times can you wink with your left eye?' 'Can you whistle?' 'Click your fingers?' 'Try something new?' 'Can you draw shapes or letters with different body parts?' 'How many body parts can take your weight?' 'What can you balance on?' 'Can you hold a pose?' Explorations of facial expressions, sensory experiences and whole body movement associated with feelings (e.g. happy, angry, etc.) can also be engaging for young learners. Using a range of different types of music such as folk, classical and pop, or sound effects, can also fuel a range of responses.

Toys, props and objects

Young learners respond very well to toys, props and objects where they build on their play experiences by exploring the toys, props and objects with whole-body movement and by

---

■ **Table 3.3** Examples of ways in which body parts can be used

Face	Lifting eyes, moving eyebrows, blinking, winking, closing eyes, wiggling nose, blowing raspberries with lips, whistling, showing tongue, smiling, frowning, exploring facial expressions
Neck and head	Carefully placing ear to shoulder, looking left, right, up, down, nodding, shaking
Shoulders	Rolling forwards and backwards
Trunk	Bending forwards, backwards, side to side, twisting
Arms	Swinging, circling, flapping, shaking, stretching
Legs	Bend, straighten, kick, shake, cross, sit, lay down
Hands and fingers	Make a fist, stretch out, shake, wiggle, flap, rub, wring, clap, click, clapping simple beats, syllables in name, keeping a beat, simple rhythm patterns
Feet and toes	Curl, stretch, point, wiggle, stand, on ball of feet, heels, tapping

---

using different body parts. Using props and objects develops *object control*. When introducing a toy, prop or object, it is helpful to consider these three related questions:

What does it look like? Here, the visual impression is important because it will engage the young learner in making sense of the prop or object, by making connections to words, objects or experiences that he or she knows from which he or she can build. For example, does it look like anything, or remind us of anything in particular?

How does it feel? Here, the tactile response will relate to the whole-body movement responses. For example, if the prop or object is a feather, children may use words such as 'light' to describe how it feels and are more likely then to show lightness in their movement responses.

What can I do with it/what can it do/how can it move? This question will engage young learners in exploring with the prop or object and their bodies. For example, they will be finding out:

■ how easy it is to move or manipulate the prop or object;
■ if the prop or object moves as they expected;
■ if the prop or object can move fast or slow;
■ where and how the prop or object moves in the space, either close to the body or in the wider space;
■ the movements and shapes the prop or object can make;
■ the weight of the prop or object – whether it is heavy or light; and
■ the flow of the prop or object – whether it is fluid or sharp/sudden.

Language to describe the look, feel and movement of the toy, prop or object can be generated by young learners and adults together. This can be oral, or a record can be made by using large pieces of paper and pens, whiteboards or iPads, if available. Table 3.4 lists a range of props and objects that are helpful for developing whole-body movement responses.

■ **Table 3.4** Examples of props and objects for developing movement and dance (not in any particular order)

Prop or object

Material in different sizes, colours and textures (e.g. silk, lycra, hessian, cotton, viscose, elastic)
Ribbons/streamers in different sizes and colours
Scarves in different sizes, colours and textures
Balls of different sizes, colours and textures
Bubbles
Bean bags
Coloured dots/spots
Pom-poms
Feathers
Shells
Coloured stones
Various musical instruments

Scenario (object control)

In a hall space, a group of children from a Year 1 class were each given a bright yellow feather. They held it, felt it and looked closely at it. Together with their teacher, they generated words and vocabulary around the three questions as starting points. The children then found their own space and worked individually as they played with the feather. They batted and bounced it on a hand, moved it between hands, threw it into the air and caught it, threw it into the air and turned; they jumped with the feather, rolled with the feather, blew the feather to keep it up or to make it go higher; they balanced it on different body parts and watched it fly and float to the ground. Next, the teacher asked the children to try out various challenges such as travelling with the feather, jumping, turning, balancing and finding their favourite movements. In later sessions, the children chose the favourite movements that they wished to show. The class watched each other show their movements with the feather. The teacher commented on the work and reinforced action words, descriptive vocabulary such as turn, stretch, roll, float, smooth and light, and discussed how the children managed to look after (control) their feather and what was easy or tricky about this. At the end of each session, the children were asked, 'What did you do today?' Here are a few of the children's replies:

'We played with feathers and made movements like a feather.'
'My feather is soft and smooth and fluffy and there are lines in it and there are stripes on it.'
'I can blow it, I can push it, I can pull it.'
'I can balance it, I can throw it, I can catch it, I can bounce it.'
'I floated like a feather.'

Children can also bring favourite toys and consider how they move/might move. Here, it is the use of actions and quality or dynamics of the movement that is most interesting (e.g. the way a robot toy is likely to move is in a stiff, jerky, sharp way, whereas, in contrast, a rag doll may be more fluid or smooth).

Scenario (locomotion/balance stability)

A group of Year 2 children were carefully considering the questions (What does it look like? How does it feel? What can I do with it/what can it do/how does it move?) in relation to a group of toys that consisted of a wind-up robot, a rag doll, a string puppet, a spinning top and a toy car. As the children considered the questions, they immediately started manipulating the toys and moving like the toys. The teacher supported language and movement development by demonstrating actions and asking questions such as:

'Does the robot move in a stiff or floppy way?'
'How would a robot move in the space?'
'Does the spinning top move fast or slow?'
'How tricky is it to stop if you spin fast?'

Such use of language is important in developing the quality or dynamics of movements in dance activities. An important aspect of teaching dance creatively is to use language and imagery in order to enhance understanding, dynamics and the quality of responses.

Bears

This theme lends itself to using a range of children's literature to support exploration of actions, space and varying the range of movement. There are many wonderful children's picture books that have a bear or bears as central characters: sleepless bears, hungry bears, lost bears, magical bears, wise bears, brave bears, lonely bears and space traveller bears. Creative movement and dance activities can be related to the theme and narrative structure of the text (e.g. in terms of rhythm or repetition) and/or by using related props relevant to the text. Particular actions, space, dynamics/quality and relationships can be explored and developed. Table 3.5 is a list of children's picture books about bears (not in any particular order) that lend themselves to further exploration through dance activities.

Here are three ways of using a children's picture book to stimulate, develop and support movement/dance activities and literacy/language:

Response: Take the children on an adventure inside the text in order to enable words, images, actions and responses to become more meaningful through creation and repetition of a physical response to theme, events, structures and words/phrases. This enables learners to explore the meaning of the text kinaesthetically, thereby aiding, for example, sequencing, language development and movement vocabulary development. Learners can then experiment with language and action by finding inventive ways.

Rhythm: Create simple chants/rhythms/rhymes. The repetitive phrases in many children's texts combined with movement patterns can develop rhythmical understanding/ pulse/phrases and internalisation of the action and the language structure.

Repetition: To develop movement quality, play around with the movement dynamics/ qualities and different uses of the body and voice to develop greater creative responses and meaning making.

■ **Table 3.5** Children's picture books about bears

Bear	Raymond Briggs
We're Going on a Bear Hunt	Michael Rosen and Helen Oxenbury
Where's My Teddy?	Jez Alboorough
This is the Bear	Sarah Hayes
Brown Bear, Brown Bear, What Can You See?	Eric Carle
The Little Mouse, the Red Ripe Strawberry and the Big Hungry Bear	Don and Audrey Wood
The Bravest Ever Bear	Allan Alhberg and Paul Howard
Bear's Best Friend	Lucy Coats
Whatever Next!	Jill Murphy
Threadbear	Mick Inkpen
Can't You Sleep Little Bear?	Martin Waddell and Barbara Firth
Bear Snores On	Karma Wilson and Jane Chapman

We're Going on a Bear Hunt

Michael Rosen   Helen Oxenbury

■ **Figure 3.1** *We're Going on a Bear Hunt*

Times of the day

Learners could explore associated movements for times of the day such as waking up time
– stretching, brushing teeth, washing, putting on clothes and so on. They could also explore
busy times such as playtime – shaking, travelling, jumping, playing with toys – and
playground games such as tag, hop scotch, skipping, clapping games and hide and seek.
Quiet time could be bedtime – stretching using different body parts in different directions,
different types of rolling, lying down and fidgeting. The children could make a phrase of
movements for each time and link the three times together. Different speeds and use of
space can be incorporated – medium speed for waking up, faster for busy and slow for
bedtime.

Weather

This could be linked to the forest school (see Chapter 9), where learners are encouraged
to put on their wellington boots and travel in and around, as well as splash, jump and
stamp in puddles – a puddle dance could be developed. An excerpt from the film *Singing*

■ **Figure 3.2** *Where's My Teddy?*

in the Rain could be used here. Learners could explore further actions in relation to rain, such as sharp and staccato-like pitter-patter raindrops – movements using body parts and the whole body. Similarly, actions and qualities in relation to the sun could be developed – calm, slow, soft, warm qualities.

The use of stimuli and themes that are meaningful to and excite the imagination of the learner are effective ways to engage with and create creative and playful dance activities and compositions.

Within the creative dance activities and starting points outlined earlier in this chapter, young learners are able to draw on Rudolph Laban's model of movement analysis/key components of dance. Laban categorises movement in four ways: action, space, dynamics/quality and relationships. Laban's work is explained in greater depth in the next chapter, but generally his work can be categorised as follows in Table 3.6.

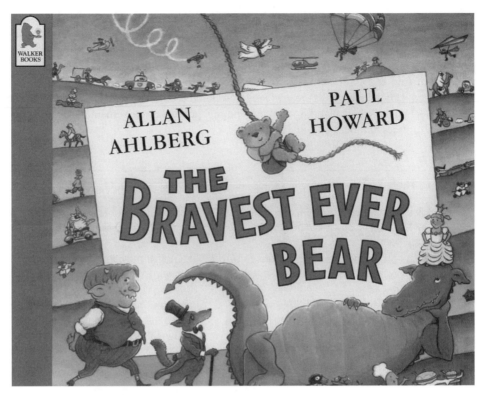

■ **Figure 3.3** *The Bravest Ever Bear*

A focus on the *action* category incorporates the basic dance actions of travel, jump, turn, stillness/balance and use of gesture, the use of different body parts, and language development through generating words and imagery to describe different body actions.

A focus on the *space* category incorporates the use of personal space and wider space, use of different directions, different pathways, body shapes, size, and high, medium or low levels in movement.

■ **Table 3.6** Laban's categories

ACTION	What can my body do?
SPACE	Where can my body move?
DYNAMICS/QUALITY/EFFORT	How can my body move?
RELATIONSHIPS	With what or whom can I move?

A focus on *dynamics or effort* incorporates changes in speed (fast/slow), weight (heavy/light) and flow (sharp/fluid) of movement. These also relate to expressive qualities in movement.

A focus on *relationships* incorporates relationships to props/objects, as well as child to child and adult/child.

Of course, the categories are interrelated, but it can be helpful to take the categories separately when planning and facilitating particular movement/dance activities. Some examples can be found in Table 3.7.

▨ **Table 3.7** Using Laban's categories to plan movement/dance activities

Focus on **actions** travel, jump, turn, gesture, stillness; different body actions; body parts	Examples: stretching, curling, reaching, twisting, turning, slither, gallop, shuffle, crawl
Focus on **space** directions; levels; size; pathways; general or personal space; body shapes	Examples: moving, stopping, forwards, backwards, diagonally, between, under, above
Focus on **dynamics/qualities/effort** changing time or speed; changing weight; changing the flow	Examples: time – fast/slow, sudden, gradual; weight – strong/delicate/gentle, heavy/light, floppy/stiff; flow – fluid/free, controlled/bound; moods and feelings – happy, sad, excited
Focus on **relationships** to peers (e.g. dancing in pairs), relationships to props (e.g. objects, toys, costumes)	Examples: hold, hug, push, pull

Planning for creative movement/dance activities

In planning for creative movement/dance activities, we are focusing on the learner's experience and learning. It is important, therefore, that we consider what the learners already know, have experienced and can do, and to use children's interests and concerns as foundations from which to build a vast array of exciting and motivating opportunities.

Here is an example of a unit of work, 'We're Going on a Bear Hunt', which is particularly suitable for introducing dance activities to Foundation Stage/Key Stage 1.

Foundation Stage/Key Stage One We're Going on a Bear Hunt
'We're Going on a Bear Hunt' Michael Rosen and Helen Oxenbury
Links to Foundation Stage – what to develop creatively:

Opportunities for the children to show appropriate control and co-ordination in large and small movements.
Opportunities to explore and move confidently in a range of ways.

Opportunities to show an awareness of space, adjusting speed and direction purposefully and negotiating small and large spaces successfully and safely. Opportunities to handle and manipulate props and equipment confidently and effectively.

Intended learning outcomes
Composition (Active learning)

Playing and exploring with:

- a range of action words
- body shapes and use of body parts
- space and speed
- moods and feelings in dance

Creating and thinking critically by:

- imitating, recalling and practising movement
- developing simple phrases of movement
- ordering movements
- developing stillness
- showing greater awareness of space by adjusting speed and direction

Performing
Playing and exploring through:

- sharing and showing ideas
- developing control of movement
- beginning to move rhythmically

Appreciation

- showing what they have done
- copying an action from someone else that they like
- using some movement and descriptive vocabulary in order to talk about observations and experiences
- talking about moods and feelings in dance

Resources

- large coloured circles/squares
- 'We're Going on a Bear Hunt' book (by Michael Rosen and Helen Oxenbury)
- percussion instruments
- props related to text:
    - long grass (long peacock feathers or ribbons)
    - mud (wellington boots)

- river (blue metallic/stretchy fabric)
- forest (leaves, range of obstacles such as bean bags and hoops)
- snow storm (white confetti/bubbles)
- bed (large fabric/blanket/parachute)

Possible dance structure – how to develop movement creatively
Warm-up ideas:

- In a circle – follow my leader – warming up large body parts and small body parts – shaking, rubbing, twisting, wiggling, stamping, bouncing, side stepping, galloping, etc.
- Using large coloured circles/squares – green for grass, brown for mud, blue for river, white for snow. Introduce just two colours/ places at a time. Lay a number of the coloured circles/squares around the room. Play travelling around the room and either say 'find . . . grass, etc.' And all the children find the correct colour.
- Travelling around the room – explore and play with different ways of walking (e.g. giant and tiny steps, stamp and tip toe).

Main section/dance ideas for imaginative exploration and composition
Introduce related props and explore the use of:

- Peacock feathers/ribbons as related to **long grass** – (using arm and hand gestures) tickly, soft, floppy, swish, sway, bend.
- Wellington boots as related to **mud** – (different types of jumping) stamp, stomp, tap, squelch – bend knees and use arms to increase height.
- Fabric as related to **river** – (extending and stretching) reaching, splash, splosh, push, pull.
- Leaves and obstacles as related to **forest** – (bending) crunch, crinkle, crack, travelling over, under, around and through.
- White confetti/bubbles as related to **snowstorm** – float, pop, light, twist, turn.
- Large fabric/parachute as related to **bed** – (laying down/hiding, being still and quiet).

Appreciation

- Children sharing and showing what they have done either as a whole class or half and half.
- Opportunities to copy an action from someone else that they like.
- Opportunities to use some movement and descriptive vocabulary in order to talk about observations and experiences.
- Opportunities to talk about moods and feelings in dance.

Development

- Use chorus as repetitive and rhythmic text and introduce related actions. These can be suggested by the practitioner or explored by the children.

■ We're going on a bear hunt (e.g. marching, galloping, following the leader).
■ We're going to catch a big one (e.g. make a large shape).
■ What a beautiful day (e.g. stretching up to the ceiling).
■ We're not scared (e.g. make a scared shape and face).

Performance – a rhythmic adventure

■ Go on a Bear Hunt adventure either inside or outside and create part or whole of the narrative with props or just actions and chorus.
■ Go on a different Hunt type of adventure linked to the children's current interests (e.g. a Giant Hunt, an Alien Hunt).

Cool down ideas

■ Tip toeing away from bear to house and bed.
■ Tired adventurers – using the blanket or parachute settle underneath to sleep, try deep breathing to relax after big adventure.
■ Become as still and quiet as possible. Practitioner taps each individual to sit up.

In order to plan a session for movement/dance, it may be worthwhile considering where the session will take place, as movement/dance activities do not have to take place in a hall space, but could be inspired by an outside site such as a forest/wood. For example, many schools now have access to 'forest school environments', and many of the children's books about bears, as discussed earlier, are set in a forest/wood, so lend themselves beautifully to exploration in a similar space. Further discussion of forest school environments can be found in Chapter 9. To aid planning a movement/dance session, consideration of particular phases of a lesson or way of working may be useful.

Introduction: Here is an opportunity to outline the theme, stimulus, activities and possible foci of the session. Movement can be stimulated in a variety of ways, as emphasised earlier in this chapter.

Warm-up: This is an opportunity to engage learners in physically moving. There could be a focus on large body parts, smaller body parts and cardiovascular work. Opportunities for travelling in a larger or unusual space with obstacles can be incorporated here. Playing with different speeds and ways of stopping and starting movement can also be helpful.

Creative movement opportunities (exploration): When developing compositions, children can play, explore and use their imagination. Developing confidence to explore and play with movement and to make and apply decisions is important. In the Physical Education curriculum, words such as 'strategies' and 'tactics' are used; although this may not seem as relevant for dance, this can be viewed more as applying problem-solving skills and using knowledge, experience and imagination.

Development of movement material (investigating and problem-solving): Select, develop and structure movement material.

Performance opportunities: With young children, this refers to developing opportunities to share and show work in progress, as well as a product. Opportunities can aid the development of bodily awareness such as being able to show stillness, exaggerate a gesture, travel in a particular pathway, extend a body part or express an emotion through movement.

Appreciation opportunities: When appreciating, learners can watch, identify, copy and begin to describe their own work and the work of others. At this age, most pupils will show what they have seen and will build towards articulating their responses.

Cool-down: Relevant props can be used for cool-downs, as well as main sessions such as a parachute or stretchy fabric. Opportunities to calm and relax the body and close the session can be used here.

Observation and assessment

Observation of responses to movement/dance activities will also include talk-based opportunities as children begin to consider what they are doing, have done and will do. Types of physical responses and talk that can be observed include making connections to previous learning, exploratory and investigative, reasoning and justification of choices made, explanation and agreement/disagreement. Creative practitioners can support and facilitate physical and talk responses by using different types of questions. Examples are included in Table 3.8.

▨ **Table 3.8** Types of questions

Open Questions	What did you like? Why? Which part did you enjoy most? What did you do? How did you do that? How could it be done? Can you try this . . .? Can you see . . . a change in speed?
Probing Questions	How did you feel when . . .? What makes you feel that? In what way? Show me/tell me more . . . Why is that an important movement? What helps you do that?
Reflective Questions	So, are you doing this? Is it this way? Is it important to do this in this way?

As young learners respond physically and orally they will build their descriptive vocabulary. Here is an example of descriptive vocabulary development that can be used for all Physical Education:

Reception

■ New words to describe different types of travelling movement (e.g. *slither, gallop, shuffle, roll, crawl*).

■ Words associated with actions (e.g. *lead, follow, copy*).

■ Different body parts.

■ Language of negotiation and cooperation (e.g. *share, wait, before, after*).

■ Different directions (e.g. *backwards, sideways, forwards*).

■ Words to describe moods and feelings (e.g. *happy, excited, sad*).

■ Words to describe different body actions (e.g. *stretching, curling, reaching, twisting, turning*).

■ Words to describe the nature of movement (e.g. *strong, gentle, heavy, floppy*).

■ Words to describe space (e.g. *between, through, above*).

■ Words that express opinions (e.g. *like, dislike*).

Year 1

■ Words to describe travel and stillness (e.g. *gallop, skip, jump, hop, bounce, spring, turn, spin, freeze, statue*).

■ Words to describe direction (e.g. *forwards, backwards, sideways*).

■ Words to describe space (e.g. *near, far, in and out, on the spot, own, beginning, middle, end*).

■ Words to describe moods and feelings (expressive qualities) (e.g. *jolly, stormy*).

■ Words to describe the nature of movement (dynamic qualities) (e.g. *fast, strong, gentle*).

Year 2

■ Words to describe body actions and body parts.

■ Words to describe levels (e.g. *high, medium, low*).

■ Words to describe directions.

■ Words to describe pathways (e.g. *curved, zigzag*).

■ Words to describe moods, ideas and feelings (e.g. *happy, angry, calm, excited, sad, lonely*).

■ Words to describe health and fitness (e.g. *tired, hot, sweaty, heart rate, warm up, cool down*).

A useful way of assessing young learners' responses in movement and dance can be to use an 'I can' chart in relation to what the child can do and how he or she can do it. An example is given in Table 3.9.

■ **Table 3.9** 'I can' movement and dance

Action	I can show lots of different movements – run, hop, skip, jump. I can move safely and stop quickly. I can copy simple actions. I can remember simple actions and repeat them. I am able to remember a sequence of two or three movements.
Space	I can show movement using big spaces and small spaces. I can travel in different directions. I can explore pathways in the space and on the floor.
Dynamics	I can show fast and slow movements. I can match movements to music and sounds. I can show different feelings through movements.
Relationships	I can handle a prop with increasing control. I can watch someone else in my group and copy what he or she does.

SUMMARY

This chapter has suggested and explored a range of suggested themes and stimuli as ways of introducing creative dance, which have included opportunities within and across the curriculum for children in the Foundation Stage and at Key Stage 1. We have argued that dance is an art form that cultivates the physical, creative, cognitive, emotional, social and artistic development of children. Use of narrative and imagery to enhance creative movement composition has been demonstrated, and Rudolph Laban's (1948, 1966, 1984) categories of movement as body awareness and actions – spatial awareness, effort/dynamics/qualities and relationships – has been introduced. Ways of planning and assessing have also been examined.

The next chapter, 'Developing dance', focuses on opportunities that are suggested as being more suited to children at Key Stage 2.

This chapter applies the POWER principles that were introduced in Chapter 1, as valuing the creative potential of the body enables young learners to build confidence. The ideas suggested here will have *purpose* to learners as they engage in physical exploration and meaning making. The ideas are pertinent to children between 4 and 7 years, and they will build on their interests and knowledge and understanding of the world. The ideas here show how *opportunities* are harnessed within and across the curriculum, and we hope that you see the potential here for dance in all areas of learning and subjects. Children's *well-being* refers to learners feeling comfortable and confident to have a go and try new things, building on what they already know, can do and understand. If children enjoy physical movement and creation, they are more likely to associate this with positive feelings, and therefore want to do more. The *environment* that is provided must be safe, positive and motivating for children so that they may feel success in their achievements and be encouraged to *revel* in this.

FURTHER READING

Bursztyn, C. K. (ed.) (2012) *Young Children and the Arts: Nurturing Imagination and Creativity*, Charlotte, NC: Information Age Publishing.

Davies, M. (2003) *Movement and Dance in Early Childhood*, London: Sage.

Stinson, S. (1998) *Dance for Young Children: Finding the Magic in Movement*, Reston, VA: American Alliance for Health, Physical Education, Recreation, and Dance.

CHAPTER 4

DEVELOPING DANCE

INTRODUCTION

In the previous chapter, 'Introducing dance', we argued that dance is a physical activity and also an expressive art form that can develop physical, artistic, aesthetic, social, cognitive and cultural education. The focus in the last chapter was particularly on Foundation Stage and Key Stage 1 learners, with an emphasis on a holistic approach to physical development and in the provision of a range of opportunities to enable learners to increase their creative responses, physical competence and confidence. This chapter examines ways of developing knowledge, skills and understanding in relation to dance compositions and performances, as well as engaging learners in appreciating dance. The National Curriculum in England Framework (2014: 181) makes reference to dance at Key Stage 2: 'pupils should be taught to perform dances using a range of movement patterns'. In this chapter, dance moves beyond 'movement patterns', and offers opportunities for learners to experience the roles of creator, performer, audience member, critic and leader:

> **Dancing** involves learning particular dances, movements, phrases, dance techniques and developing expressive skills.
>
> **Creating** is often referred to as composing and beyond schools as choreographing. This involves the exploration, selection, rejection and refining of movement material in the construction and making of dances.
>
> **Performing** can mean a sharing of work in process or a final product. This can happen during lessons, workshops, assemblies, dance festivals, competitions or events.
>
> **Watching** is an active process and develops skills in focus, attention, concentration, observation, interpretation and critical evaluation and appreciation. This can be learners watching each other, filming and playing back work, professional dance works, dance works specifically made for film or screen, live dance in a theatre setting, live dance beyond theatre such as site-specific.
>
> (Siddall 2010: 19–20, original emphasis)

This chapter, 'Developing dance', explores ways of teaching for creative bodies and relates to the POWER principles in *purpose* by valuing purposeful physical activity, meaning-making and expressive opportunities. The *opportunities*, stimuli and ideas offered can be used within and across the curriculum. *Well-being* is valued through increased coordination, control, posture, strength, stamina, flexibility and mobility, the enjoyment of moving, and in 'making connections between feelings, values and ideas' (Siddall 2010: 9). The *environment* created in developing dance is one that values individual and group responses, encourages relationship building and is inclusive. Furthermore, the share and show opportunities initiate celebration and time to *revel* in the empowerment of physical responses to ideas and possibilities for the application of dance vocabulary, composition, performance, and appreciation knowledge, skills and understanding.

The act of dancing involves the development of technical and expressive skills where actions can be performed using different combinations of dynamics, space and relationships. Laban's *movement analysis* was introduced in the last chapter as a way of describing movement. Laban formulated his movement principles through observation of movement in different situations, as they are general principles of movement that are not just specific to dance:

> Laban's system is not codified into set patterns of movement which need to be fed to pupils according to age, ability and expertise. Rather they are progressive stages inherent in the use of the principles which Laban organised into sixteen movement themes.
>
> (Smith-Autard 2002: 18)

Laban's work is based on the premise that learners are free to explore their natural movement range 'in order to clarify steps and techniques and in order to move beyond dance steps into meaningful movement' (Bradley 2008: 12). Laban describes movement under four headings: body/action, effort/dynamics/qualities, space, and relationships.

Body/action is concerned with *what* the body does

Actions are doing words (verbs). Laban identified the following framework for action: bend, stretch and twist as the fundamental actions underpinning all movement. There are six different kinds of action (see Table 4.1).

In action, body parts could be isolated (particular body parts moving or still), emphasised so that attention was on a particular body part regardless of other actions being performed, or a body part could lead movements such as a shoulder leading a lean. Laban's analysis also offers a framework for progression, as simple movement material using single actions can be used with young children (as suggested in the previous chapter). Older groups can combine different kinds of action as layered demands of body parts.

Space is concerned with *where* movements are located

This concerns whereabouts a learner is located and moving in space.

There are 10 spatial aspects (see Table 4.2).

Spatial awareness can be developed progressively from a simple change of level with young children (as suggested in the previous chapter). Older groups can play with pathways, change the movement's size action and engage with exploring transitions.

■ Table 4.1 Six different types of action

TRAVEL (LOCOMOTION): movements from one point to another.

TURN: movements involving a change of front.

GESTURE: movements without weight-bearing body parts.

ELEVATION: movements in which the body is jumping/fighting gravity. There are five basic variations of jump:
One foot to the same foot
One foot to the other foot
One foot to two feet
Two feet to one foot
Two feet to two feet

TRANSFER OF WEIGHT (STEPPING): movements that support transfers from one part of the body to another.

STILLNESS: movements where the body is intentionally still (e.g. balance).

Source: Adapted from Tomkins (2012: 44–50)

■ Table 4.2 Spatial aspects

GENERAL/PERSONAL SPACE: the amount that movements extend into space.

SIZE: the amount of space that movements require.

PROXIMITY: movements that are close to or far away from the body, near and far.

PATHWAYS: the line, route or shape made in space.

LEVELS: low, medium and high.

DIRECTIONS, DIMENSIONS, PLANES: movements largely travel forwards towards centre front.

FACINGS: direction in which the body faces.

BODY DESIGN/SHAPE: direction in which the body faces.

SYMMETRY AND ASSYMMETRY

TRANSITIONS: how movement is linked between and through.

Source: Adapted from Tomkins (2012: 44–50)

■ Table 4.3 Effort/dynamic aspects

TIME: the length of time taken to execute body action(s) or duration.

WEIGHT: the amount of tension required in the execution of body action(s).

SPACE: the focus given to body action(s).

FLOW: the type/amount of energy.

RHYTHM: variations in time, force and flow.

PHRASING: use of pace or impact.

Source: Adapted from Tomkins (2012: 44–50)

Effort/dynamics is concerned with *how* the body moves

This concerns how movements are 'coloured' in terms of how much energy is used. Dynamic words describe how the action words are being performed (adverbs).

There are six effort/dynamic aspects (see Table 4.3).

Effort/dynamic awareness can be developed progressively from a simple change of time (speed) with young children (as suggested in the previous chapter). Older groups can combine weight, time and flow qualities.

> The dynamics of dance can be thought of rather like the colours of a painting: they create points of interest and contrast as well as expressing much of the meaning. For example, varying the speed in a dance or contrasting the use of off-balance movements that portray a sense of urgency and vitality, with balanced positions that allow the audience a moment of rest.
>
> (Pickard and Earl 2004: 113)

Every action, then, can be coloured according to how it uses time, energy, flow, space and relationship factors. Knowledge and understanding of technical development along with principles of movement can be integrated so common terms such as balance, turn and jump are used to describe movement alongside dynamic and spatial characteristics with words such as sharp, sustained, upward, backwards and so on. The use of Laban's work can be helpful in identifying, selecting and developing movement material when planning, teaching and evaluating.

Relationships is concerned with *who* or *what* the learner dances

Younger children can dance independently and/or altogether with the teacher as a whole class, whereas older children can work in pairs and groups and consider formations (see Table 4.4 below).

■ **Table 4.4** Relationship aspects

PARTNER: copy, mirror, lead, follow, meet, part, pass, action, reaction, unison, canon, opposition, under, over, around, through.
GROUP: inter-group relationships, group formations such as line, circle, scattered, etc.

Source: Adapted from Tomkins (2012: 44–50)

Creating dance is a rigorous decision-making process that involves developing a dance idea through exploration, experimentation, selecting, rejecting and refining movement and practice. Choices of movement vocabulary and the creation of phrases, motifs and sequences, as well as the structure of the dance, are all important decisions. The teaching of dance in primary schools is related to Laban's work, but also Smith-Autard's (2002: 5) 'Midway Model for Teaching Dance'. Here, there is a careful balance between an *educational model* of teaching dance and a *professional model*. The *educational model*, which was developed in the 1940s and practised until the 1970s, focused only on process, imagination, individuality, movement principles, feelings associated with moving rather than what the movement looked like, with the teacher's role as a guide. In contrast, the *professional model* of teaching dance, which was developed in the 1960s and 1970s, focused on product, objective ends, and stylistically defined techniques and theatre dance, where the emphasis was on what the movement looked like rather than how it felt, with the teacher being viewed as director and expert. Here, children were often involved in copying and learning prescribed dances and techniques. Criticisms of the educational model were that the processes of creating dance were too subjective and difficult to assess or evaluate (Smith-Autard 2002: 6), and that the *professional model* was too restrictive and lacked any creativity. The Midway Model advocates a more equal emphasis on quality processes and quality products. Here, the emphasis is on creativity, imagination and individuality, knowledge of theatre dance, feelings and objectivity, movement principles, and technical development. The three interrelated aspects of creating, performing and appreciating provide a coherent conceptual framework for the study of dance. Peter Brinson (1991: 69), although writing over 20 years ago, stated that 'the realm of dance in education of the body and the imagination'. This is still relevant today, as it advocates dance education as a physical art form.

KEY ASPECTS

In this chapter, we will focus on ways of helping learners use a range of movement vocabulary and dance skills in compositions, performance and appreciation. A variety of stimuli/starting points will be suggested, and dance vocabulary in relation to actions, qualities, space and relationships will be identified that can be used to explore, select, develop and refine movement into simple and more complex structures.

It is important to plan for continuity and progression in creative dance teaching and to build on from where learners are. For example:

■ developing single actions to simple and complex movement phrases;
■ enabled to work alone, in pairs and small groups;
■ encouraged to use and apply their knowledge, skills and developing understanding of shape, speed, size, direction, level, tension and flow;
■ articulating greater clarity of movement, strength and flexibility; and
■ expressing a range of feelings, moods and ideas, to respond stimuli.

These developmental features could also support assessment (see Table 4.5).

Here, follow two themes and stimuli for creative dance at Key Stage 2 that offer a range of ideas, as well as the structure and way of working that will aid planning and assessment. The themes/stimuli are as follows:

■ *Pathways* focuses on spatial aspects of direction, levels, use of personal and whole space, transitions, and use of shapes in space. There are opportunities for whole-class, individual, paired and group work.
■ *Chance dance* focuses on actions and movement vocabulary, use of dynamics, and compositional devices. There are opportunities for whole-class, individual and group work.

Table 4.5 Suggested continuity and progression in making, performing and evaluating dances

Making (composing) dances	Performing dances	Evaluating (appreciating) dances
Copy	Solo	Observe
Repeat	Awareness of others in a pair or group	Show
Coordination, combining and/or linking two or more movements together	Musicality	Recognise
Recall and repeat a phrase of movement	Enhancing movement memory	Describe
Select/reject movements	Practising, refining and clarifying	Discuss
Use choreographic devices such as unison, leading/following, mirroring, canon and contrast	Expression and feeling	Compare
Structure with a beginning, middle and end	Focus and projection	Suggest

After these, there are three more ideas that offer starting points for Key Stage 2 dance for you to add your own developments. These are:

■ dance from different times and places;
■ poetry; and
■ developing a motif and dance idea.

Pathways

A pathway is the route taken between two points (see Figure 4.1). It can be a straight line, curve, zigzag and so on, or a combination of these. An exploration of pathways will engage learners in developing greater spatial awareness and understanding of movement through and around a space.

Warm up

■ Starting small and growing tall as a vertical pathway or low to high level.
■ Playing follow my leader as a whole class and then, as pairs, trying circular pathways, incorporating high, medium and low levels and exploring a snaky/wiggly winding pathway.
■ Whole class are in a space and one learner is the explorer. The explorer has to make a pathway through and around all of the people in a space. The people in the space can be rocks in interesting shapes. The explorer must go around, under, over and through.

■ Try a *farandole* dance: a *farandole* is a line of people holding each other's hands. One person is the leader, and one person is the tail. The leader (at the head of the line) leads the *farandole*, as the group walk and follow the leader, making zigzags in the line. The leader must walk all the time so that the tail is also walking. It is easier, at the beginning, to place cones to identify a path, and the leader can then gently zigzag in between the cones. In an open *farandole*, the leader passes underneath the connection between the tail and the second person before the tail, leading the whole line under this human 'bridge'. The tail must remain on the spot. When the line has passed through, the second person before the tail will make the tail turn in on itself as the line goes under the tail's arm. A more advanced version is l'escargot (snail) (see Figure 4.2).

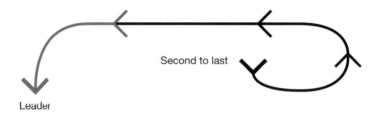

Second to last

Leader

■ **Figure 4.1** An example of a pathway

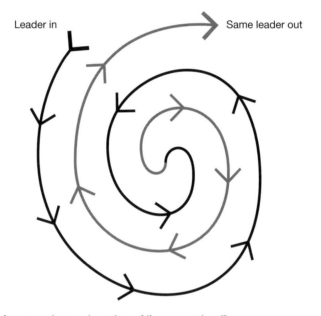

Leader in   Same leader out

■ **Figure 4.2** A more advanced version of l'escargot (snail)

Creating movement material

■ Explore circling movements through using whole body and body parts.
■ Try a variety of different turns.

- Try a variety of different rolls.
- Try circling pathways on the floor and in the air.
- Draw different pathways on a board or have pre-prepared cards with them, such as snaking, round, zigzag, diagonal, wiggly, snail (all should have been used in the warm-up – see example of a wiggly pathway in Figure 4.3).

Learners work in pairs, they choose a pathway and travel to follow it to get from a starting point to finishing point:

- Explore the movement chosen to move from a starting point to a finishing point.
- Create a partner dance based on pathways, following and leading.
- Discuss where they are travelling (e.g. the seaside, zoo, park), and ask them to show this as a freeze frame at the end of their pathway.
- Add stopping points along the pathway. What will you do at this stopping point? Balance, turn, jump, etc.

Development

Further developments and resources can be introduced to inspire, motivate and develop this work on use of pathways and space:

- Get your pairs to join together so you have groups of four, get the pairs to teach each other their pathways, and ask them to use one stop point idea from each group member.
- The groups could record their pathway in the shape of a 'map'. How could they represent their stop point actions on their 'map'? What symbol would you use to represent a turn?

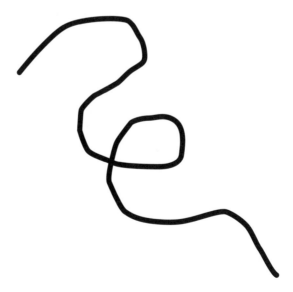

■ **Figure 4.3** A wiggly pathway

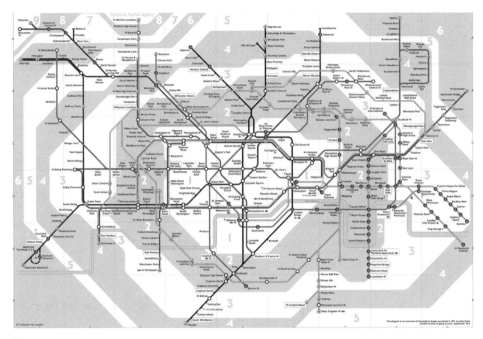

■ **Figure 4.4** Map of London Underground

- ▦ Show a map of the London Underground (see Figure 4.4 above). Each group could choose a pathway (coloured line) to explore and add to their composition.
- ▦ Another resource to use is paintings by Kandinsky (see Figure 4.5), which can also aid the quality and accuracy of the use of creative pathways and shapes.
- ▦ Learners can choose a particular shape or line to follow. Engage the children in adding contrast so some fast and slow movements, use of floor and jumps for height, and so on.
- ▦ A dance piece can be created that begins with the partner pathway piece, including the stopping points and freeze frame, meeting another pair and either engaging in the pathway piece with stopping points together or in developing the London Underground or Kandinsky pathway piece including contrast.
- ▦ Encourage the learners to be clear about the flow of the transition points between the partner into the group piece and being clear about how the piece will finish.
- ▦ Encourage the learners to be clear about the beginning, middle and end.

Performing

- ▦ Learners can perform in their groups as half the class as dancers and half as the audience, then swap, or perform a group at a time.

Appreciation

- ▦ Look carefully to see if you can tell what pathway the group are travelling along. Can you tell how they are travelling? What movements are incorporated into the

■ **Figure 4.5** Kandinsky painting

Cossacks, 1910–11, Wassily Kandinsky 1866–1944
© Tate, London 2013

stopping points? Where are they going to – can you tell from the freeze frame? What movements are used during the transition from the partner to the group piece?

■ Can contrasting movements be identified?

■ How does the piece finish?

■ Is there a clear beginning, middle and end?

Cool down

■ All stand in a space. Ask one child to walk in a winding pathway around the others. As they pass each child, they join onto the line. All travel in and out, stretching up in the middle, and down low at the outside.

■ Slowly step sideways around the circle, and reverse.

■ Stretch tall and shrink, and finish sitting on the floor.

■ Ask one pupil to lead the group back to their classroom, snaking around the room and out of the door. The *farandole* from the warm up can be incorporated here.

Chance dance

Chance dance uses random occurrence to influence the dance tasks performed. The chance element can be generated through the use of, for example:

■ dice;
■ a pack of cards/prepared cards;
■ words/a sentence chosen at random from a book/poem; and
■ numbers from a telephone number.

Each possible number/letter/word is attributed a movement/movement idea; therefore, the order that the numbers/letters/cards appear decides the order of the dance. This can help pupils generate movement orders/patterns that they would not normally come up with.

Warm up

■ In advance, a list is created that lists numbers 1–6 and a corresponding action, like so:

> 1 = travel
> 2 = turn
> 3 = jump
> 4 = gesture
> 5 = roll
> 6 = balance

■ All stand in a circle. A large die is rolled into the centre of the circle. Whichever number it lands on, the group have to do the action (i.e. 3 = any kind of jump). It may be that the teacher wants to share or teach a particular kind of jump that all try, or the learners can all do their own idea of a kind of jump.
■ Explore different types of:
    ■ *travelling* (e.g. plodding, gliding, whizzing, darting, zooming, dragging, floating, etc.).
    ■ *turning* and *rolling* (e.g. spinning, whirling, swirling, coiling, curling, spiralling, swerving, etc.).
    ■ *jumping* (e.g. bouncing, bobbing, soaring, skimming, bubbling, hopping, pouncing, etc.).
    ■ *balancing* (e.g. freezing, pausing, hesitating, suspending, interrupting, braking, etc.).
    ■ *gesturing* (e.g. tapping, flicking, shaking, quivering, flickering, jerking, pulling, pushing, pointing, waving, etc.).
These could be led by the teacher or learners. Lists of ideas could be pre-prepared as posters.
■ Explore trying the different types of actions above, paying attention to changes in speed, strength, levels and directions.
■ Choose up to six parts of the body (e.g. head, arms, legs, etc.) and write these on a whiteboard or on cards. Choose six body actions (e.g. travel, jump, turn, gesture, roll, stillness/balance) and write these on a whiteboard or on cards. As a whole class standing in a circle, the teacher or learners can choose a body part card and action card, and warm the body part up through that action (e.g. travel leading with your shoulder, turn leading with your foot, jump with your hands, etc.).

Creating movement material

Using dice:

■ Number all of the children randomly from one to six.
■ Get all of the number ones to form a group, and all of the twos, etc.
■ Get the groups to identify six movements and number them one to six.
■ Give each group a die. They must roll the die to determine which order they will perform their movements (e.g. a 1 might equal a type of balance, etc.).
■ Encourage the group to think carefully about linking movements and how the sequence flows.

Development

■ Identify movement dynamics (e.g. fast, slow, smooth, gentle, sharp, etc.). Again, pre-prepared cards can be made, or the whiteboard can be used. Each group can have two dynamic cards to add into their composition somewhere.
■ Add compositional devices, such as group formations, use of canon and unison.

Appreciation

Watch and evaluate each group sequence. Can you see which movement idea is being used? How is the order different to your order? Which order do you prefer, and why?

Cool down

■ Use the dice to bring the dance time to a close by adding more relaxed movements and stretching, for example:

1 = breathing in and a slower breath out
2 = stretch
3 = melt
4 = lay flat
5 = roll
6 = balance

Dance from different times and places

The teaching of any existing dance form will involve placing it within a social, historical and cultural context. The following questions will aid planning:

■ When and where was the dance performed?
■ What actions are typical in this dance?
■ How are they performed?
■ Are special clothes or shoes worn for this dance?

■   What is the music/accompaniment like?
■   How can the dance be developed as a creative idea/starting point for creative work?

Resources can include:

■   pictures;
■   on-screen resources;
■   step patterns;
■   music;
■   costumes; and
■   props.

This topic is vast, and lends itself to a range of possibilities. It may be that children or members of families within the school have a particular interest or knowledge of a dance style that they can share. The important point to note here is that this stimulus/starting point is not about the children learning set dances, but is an exploration of some of the key features of the dance style. A simple phrase can be shared in a particular dance style that can then be used as a starting point for learners to create their own dances inspired by the features. For example, an examination of ballet might explore turn-out, stretched feet, dancing with straight backs, unison as *corps de ballet*, and telling stories through mime and gesture, whereas African would be grounded or low to the ground through using *plié* (bent legs), use of the shoulders and upper back. Animal dance crazes related to ragtime music, and exploring some of the movements such as 'horse trot', 'kangaroo hop' and 'duck waddle' could also be developed.

Exploring features of dance styles and genres might include:

■   eras (e.g. Britain post-1930s – Lindy Hop, Rock 'n' Roll;
■   cultural/social dances: party dances, celebration, carnival;
■   step patterns: heel, toe, shuffle, hop, stomp, jump, stamp, side step, promenade;
■   hand gestures such as Asian Mudras symbols;
■   actions: travelling, jumping, turning movements;
■   partner work: ways of turning your partner, back to back, moving around your partner;
■   spatial features such as group formations, floor patterns and pathways: circle, longways set, square, lines; and
■   rhythmic structures: pulse in African, Asian, South American.

Poetry

Poetry lends itself as a stimulus for dance because, most often, they use verbs and adverbs. Moods, imagery and certain literary devices such as alliteration and onomatopoeia can also enable creative dance. Learners can create and perform dance movements to interpret the meaning of a poem. Many different types of poetry can be useful (e.g. narrative, autobiographical, haiku and rhyming). Shapes poems can be particularly useful, as they engage learners in explicit and implicit shapes and imagery.

Excerpts from the musical *Cats* by Andrew Lloyd Webber can be used to generate ideas and/or perhaps a visit from a real cat, which the learners can observe. The words presented in the shape poem (Figure 4.6) offer opportunities for an examination of body/action in relation to cat-like movements and dynamics, but use of space and relationships can also be explored.

RUNNING
WIGGLY
SOFT
JUMPING
leaping
sniffing
running
furry
MEOW
cuddly
CUDDLY
CUTE
LEAPING
Cat
JUMPING
fur
WIGGLY
SNIFFING
CUTE
CUDDLY
MEOW RUNNING

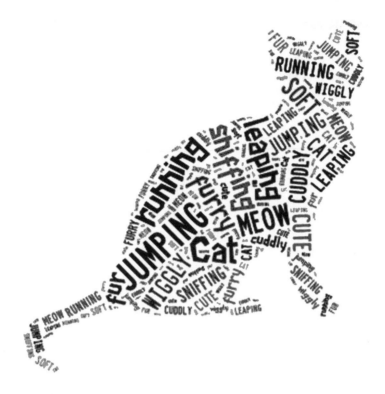

Figure 4.6 A shape poem

Image created using Tagxedo (www.tagxedo.com)

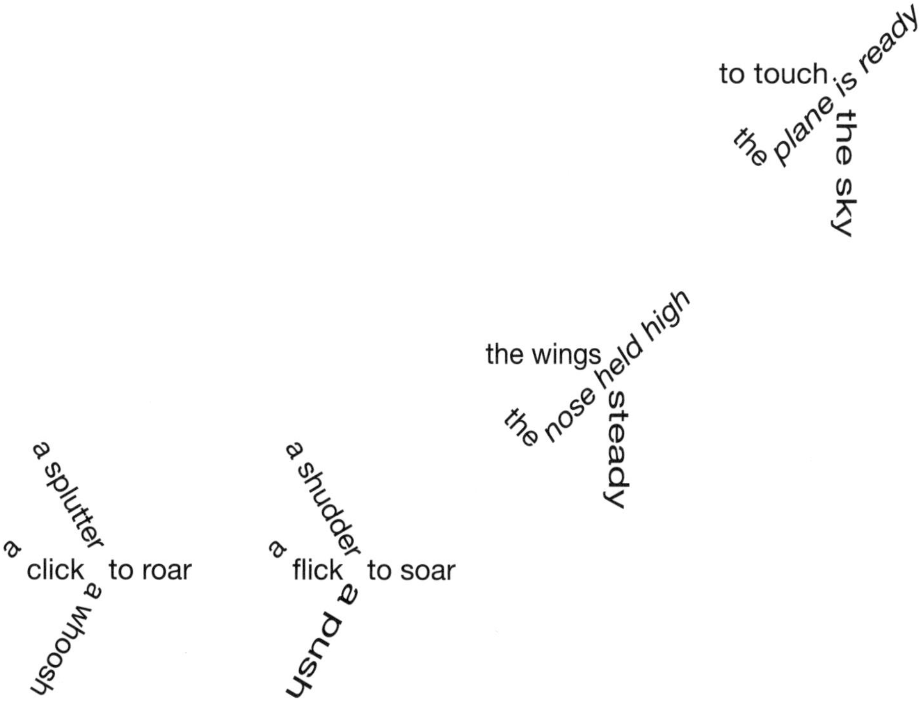

to touch
the plane is ready
the sky
the wings
the nose held high
steady
a splutter
a
click
to roar
a whoosh
a shudder
a
flick
to soar
a push

Figure 4.7 Aeroplane shape poem

The example of an aeroplane shape poem (Figure 4.7) can be used for its descriptive movement vocabulary, use of levels and/or for group choreography incorporating the aeroplane shapes in space.

At the Sea-Side
(Robert Louis Stevenson)

When I was down beside the sea
A wooden spade they gave to me
To dig the sandy shore
My holes were empty like a cup
In every hole the sea came up
Till it could come no more.

This poem 'At the Sea-Side' can be used with a number of different ages and stages, as it has such a range of potential for process and product. The poem could be used as part of a whole-class discussion about being at the beach/what can be seen/ found at the beach and/or this can relate to work being experienced at beach school (see Chapter 9). Children can engage in an analysis of the structure, word choices, imagery, mood, and the features of rhythm, rhyme and repetition. During the exploration of vocabulary, learners can examine actions, dynamics, space and relationships to create shapes, movements and phrases. Travelling actions in relation to waves and the movement of the tide and sea, showing forwards and backwards, up and down, and curved and circular spatial patterns and pathways can also be explored. Each line of the poem can be interpreted through action and movements, and phrases created and linked. Concentration could be on the verse, with the words read aloud, and recorded with certain lines repeated. The children could maintain this structure or select, reject and change the position, or repeat certain lines of the poem in the dance. This work can be undertaken by individuals, pairs or groups.

Some further suggestions might be to explore:

▪ use of breath – try breathing in and out with control, then big breaths in and slow and soft breaths out;
▪ stretching and rising up while breathing in and releasing when breathing out;
▪ gentle, flowing movements using large and small body parts like ripples in the sea;
▪ particular actions such as sways, swings, rolls and spiral turns;
▪ symmetrical and asymmetrical shapes; and
▪ different ways of travelling.

To develop the piece further, a greater awareness of sudden and sustained, and strong and light movements can be developed. Phrases of movement can be sequenced, such as gentle ripples contrasted with strong, active travelling movements as the sea crashes against the shore can be created. Use of particular vocabulary in relation to body actions can be used to enhance the execution of movements:

▪ Travel – *drift, drag, meander, glide, float, hurtle, spring.*
▪ Turn – *swirl, swing, whip, spiral, roll.*
▪ Jump – *bounce, bob, flip, spurt.*

■ Down – *dive, slide, crash.*
■ Gesture – *ripple, reach.*

(Pickard and Earl 2004)

Developing a motif and dance idea

In order to develop movement material and choreography, there are some simple strategies (motif development) you can use. A *motif* is a single movement or a short movement phrase that stems from your original dance idea. It can be used as a source or spark from which the rest of the movement develops, and is useful for creative dance-making, particularly at the latter part of Key Stage 2. Keep your motif simple and use it as a starting point; let us say, for example, that the stimulus/starting point was everyday or pedestrian movement, such as walking, running, stopping, waving, falling, glancing, brushing hair, brushing teeth, getting dressed and so on. A single movement or short phrase of movement (motif) could be developed based on actions, such as ×6 walks (e.g. as though walking to school). This could be ×3 slow, ×3 fast. Now add ×2 waiting gestures as though waiting for a bus. Spatial aspects could be added to the phrase, such as adding a pathway for the walks and a medium-level and low-level waiting gesture, and weight qualities considered, such as ×3 slow, rhythmic and ×3 frenzied walks and a heavy quality to the gestures. Adding different music or sound could add interest and change the dynamics of the phrase, such as trying the phrase to:

■ a whisper;
■ voices – chanting, babbling, loud, soft;
■ percussion – range of instruments, exploring qualities of sounds, creating movement responses to sound;
■ different styles of music;
■ environmental sounds; and
■ different rhythms.

Once you have created a motif, you can develop it and change it in the following ways:

Repetition

■ Exactly the same.
■ Use the other side of the body to start.
■ Change the order.
■ Face a different front.
■ Perform it backwards.

Variation

■ Change the speed of the motif or of one action.
■ Change the direction of the motif or of one action.
■ Change the level.
■ Change the size.

Development

■ Add in a new action.
■ Take away one action.
■ Change the floor pattern.
■ Keep the arm actions, but vary the leg and foot actions.
■ Incorporate pauses.
■ Use a different part of the body to perform the motif.

With a partner, perform the motif . . .

■ Facing your partner.
■ Side by side with partner.
■ With some contact.
■ Mirroring your partner.
■ Using a question-and-answer format.
■ Each using different levels.

In a group, perform the motif . . .

■ In unison (all together at the same time).
■ In canon.
■ Leading and following (select a leader or group of leaders).
■ Facing alternate directions.
■ Close or far from each other.
■ While entering or exiting the stage.

One creative task could be to ask learners to repeat and vary the motif by changing it in two/three ways, but there is much potential here.

SUMMARY

This chapter examined ways of developing knowledge, skills and understanding in relation to dance compositions and performances, as well as engaging learners in appreciating dance. Laban's *Movement Analysis* was explored in more depth in relation to body/action, dynamics, space and relationships, and Smith-Autard's *Midway Model for Teaching Dance*, and the interrelated aspects of creating, performing and appreciating were discussed. We argue that creating dance is a rigorous decision-making process. A variety of stimuli/starting points have been suggested and examined, as well as the importance of continuity and progression as an aid to planning and assessment. There are a plethora of ideas to use as starting points for dance, including many cross-curricular opportunities. Let us return to the POWER principles – this chapter has demonstrated the *purpose* of physical exploration and meaning-making, and such investigation and problem-solving enables the learner to gain greater understanding of his or her body. Dance lends itself beautifully to many cross-curricular links – in this chapter, there are connections to geography and art in pathways, maths in chance dance, history and music in dance from different times and places, and literacy in poetry. There is potential for many more links, which we hope you will enjoy making. *Opportunities* in dance enable learners to progress and achieve their potential. Learners experience *well-being* and pleasure associated with moving, and the beneficial effects such as greater strength, fitness, coordination, stamina and confidence. Central to valuing and developing creativity is the idea of 'creativity in relationship' (Chappell *et al.* 2009). The learners and practitioner are engaged in an *environment* where building and developing skills of negotiating relationships as they investigate and problem-solve together is positive. Learners also take on a range of roles, from creator to critic. Children can *revel* and celebrate physical, social, emotional and cognitive successes.

FURTHER READING

Laban, R. (2011) *The Mastery of Movement*, fourth edition, revised by L. Ullmann, Alton: Dance Books.

Sanders, L. (ed.) (2013) *Dance Teaching and Learning: Shaping Practice*, second edition, London: Youth Dance England.

Siddall, J. (2010) *Dance in and Beyond Schools*, London: Youth Dance England.

Smith-Autard, J. (2002) *The Art of Dance in Education*, second edition, London: A & C Black.

CHAPTER 5

INTRODUCING GYMNASTIC ACTIVITIES

INTRODUCTION

This chapter is about creative teaching and learning through the introductory curriculum of gymnastic activities for all children aged between 4 and 7 years. It is about enhancing all attributes of children's physical literacy through providing opportunities for increasing physical competence in fundamental movement patterns established in infancy and early years, towards the attainment of motor skill maturity and for promoting independent learning and achievement. 'Gymnastics gives scope for ingenuity, versatility, adaptability as well as efficient body management, agility, acrobatics and creativity' (Maude 2001: 108).

The primary school years are the 'skill-hungry' years when children are eager to 'do', to be successful, to gain mastery of the body, to learn new skills, and to be agile, coordinated and articulate movers. As suggested by DES (1972), increasing skill leads them 'to do impossible things in impossible ways'. The majority of children enjoy physical activity, thus providing the teacher with a captive and eager audience; they are ready to work hard, use their boundless energy and enjoy their learning. It is both a privilege and a responsibility for the teacher to work with children in Key Stage 1 (ages 5–7), to capitalise on their exuberance and their latent ability to learn, and to build on their unique physical and movement development, knowledge and understanding, motivation and confidence.

Children bring with them to school a rich movement vocabulary, emanating from the vast range of experience of moving to learn and learning to move that permeated their preschool experience.

The school curriculum of activities for children aged 4–7 years (foundation stage), which leads into gymnastics for children aged 7–11 years, is based on the two themes of *locomotion* and *stability*. These have been previously proposed by Gallahue (cited in Bailey and Macfadyen 2000: 78) and recreated by the Youth Sport Trust (2012) in *Start to Move*. These two themes of locomotion and stability support children's sensorimotor and neuromotor development, helping them to gain increased motor control, stability in stillness and movement, coordination, body management, spatial awareness, and a greater understanding of general fitness in relation to strength, flexibility and stamina.

The unique learning environment for introducing gymnastic activities normally consists of a large, open, indoor space, which enables children to move freely, with a clean floor, so that they can work in bare feet and learn to use the range of large and small apparatus arranged around the sides of the space, ready to be incorporated into the learning environment during each session. These together present new opportunities for exploration, discovery and challenge, and are stimuli for successful learning and achievement. Locomotion and stability activities not only enhance learners' knowledge and understanding of ways of moving in different situations, but also of applying and adapting movement from one situation to another. They can also be used to promote ways of gaining confidence in what can be achieved, can encourage children to invest in trial and error, movement selection and rejection, repetition and practice, to cooperate with others, to accept and work with the teacher's creative challenges, and to learn through discovery. Building the learning around increasing movement vocabulary, developing movement memory and enhancing movement quality gives learners the greatest range of opportunities for an all-round experience. Learners can acquire and develop movement vocabulary, select and apply this, and then evaluate and improve their performance.

KEY ASPECTS

Stability

One of the key elements in the curriculum is knowledge and application of stability. This involves achieving balance and control in both still and moving situations, as can be seen when watching experienced gymnasts performing what appear to be complex skills and sequences of movement, with coordination, poise and apparent ease. The fundamental motor skill of standing still is an example of stability. Promoting and ensuring articulate postural development in young children contributes not only to physical competence, but also aids cognitive, social and emotional development (Goddard-Blythe 2012). Managing to control their standing posture, to hold a straight, vertical, symmetrical and still position with poise, can seem to be an almost insurmountable challenge to many young children.

Scenario

Can every child in your class stand on one foot, maintaining the hips in a horizontal position, without wobbling or losing control in the arms or upper body?

Are those children who cannot maintain their posture on one foot and start to wobble also seen to be trying to compensate by waving their arms or hands around, or by displaying facial gestures, tongue activity or other contortions in the body? These indications of the severity of the challenge that the child is experiencing inevitably lead to loss of control in various parts of the body, and to failure to achieve a still standing position on one foot.

How can this be overcome? In former times, it was felt that more practice was all that was required, but how many times can a child be exposed to repeated failure before giving up altogether, particularly when that failure is based on physical immaturity? The principle of 'moment of readiness' is directly applicable in this instance, whereby success is achieved when the learner has developed both the necessary physical ability and cognitive understanding of the task and its constituent elements. Creative teaching of balance offers learning experiences that directly address this challenge, by enabling children to explore a movement vocabulary of progressive activities that develop their

---

body and spatial awareness, in order to control both their standing posture and all other positions that they choose to make. In these ways, both sensorimotor and neuromotor development can be greatly enhanced, and learners gain opportunities to extend their physical and movement development in stimulating, absorbing and beneficial ways.

Locomotion

This is the second key element in the curriculum, and is important in contributing to the mastery of core movement skills, particularly in enhancing gait, stepping patterns, and the efficient use of feet and postural management in walking, running and other travelling actions. Locomotion on the feet also includes development of jumping, while exploration of agility enables learners to explore locomotion on other parts of the body in order to develop increased coordination, movement competence, and knowledge and understanding of movement applications in performance.

Scenario

Observe the children in your class as they walk about the classroom or run freely outdoors. Are the feet used fully, from heel to toe, with the feet pointing forwards as they step? Is the posture upright with the head facing forwards, to avoid twists and turns in the body? Are the shoulders held squarely so that the arms swing with control, forwards and backwards in opposition to the feet (as the left foot steps, the right arm swings forward)? Is the whole action relaxed, rhythmic, streamlined and resilient? Does the learner remain streamlined, resilient and rhythmic when running? Further detail can be seen in Maude (2003). One of the challenges for the creative teacher is to devise opportunities for learners to achieve efficient locomotion, both when they are walking at slow pace and when they are travelling at speed.

For learners newly arrived in school, the anticipation of 'going to the hall' can be both 'scary' and very exciting. There is much to find out and learn about locomotion and stability, and about how to access activities using the floor, mats and apparatus. Add to these the challenges of managing the space, cooperating with all those sharing that same space and developing movement vocabulary, movement memory and movement quality, and the creative teacher will have plenty of discovery experience to offer. Management issues, such as the school's routine for changing and storing clothes, socks and shoes, making a class line, and walking from the classroom to the hall and back, will all have been practised in advance of the first session, so that organisational details that are a separate part of movement experience do not intervene in the enjoyment of the first learning experience in movement towards gymnastics. Preparing the hall in advance of the first session will also enable learners to ease with a sense of security into their work. For example, coloured spots (throw down markers) or individual mats could be spread out in spaces all over the hall floor so that when the learners arrive, they can find a spot or mat to stand on with tidy posture, ready to begin. Alternatively, if spots or mats have been placed in the four corners of the hall, learners can walk to pick up a spot or mat, place it in a space and then stand in a symmetrical, tidy posture, ready to start. Walking, marching, jogging, bouncing and hopping on the spot or mat, with stopping to regain breath and check posture, makes a secure, readily accessible and highly active, yet successful and controlled, first task.

The importance of getting out of breath can also be established. Finding and practising ways to get off and onto the spot or mat, as well as going around it and across it on the feet, adds further challenge to locomotion. Working within their own personal space to begin with avoids the confusion sometimes caused by having to travel through the entire hall space, negotiating everyone else as they go. Making shapes on the spot or mat gives the learners opportunities to show what they can do when stretching into wide and long shapes and then folding down into small, tucked shapes. Contrasting locomotion and shape-making on the learner's own spot or mat allows for concentration on the movement in hand, with maximum time on task, again avoiding the additional challenge of moving cooperatively with others through the entire space. Choosing and showing a favourite way to travel and a favourite shape to make then enables learners to begin to evaluate their own activity and select what they wish to share. A helpful administrative by-product of this approach with learners working in one place is that the teacher can more easily see each learner and more readily assess abilities and responses and give focused feedback. Focused feedback, to help the learner build confidence, knowledge and performance, can very beneficially be made up of three valuable ingredients, namely:

1   Praise – 'Well done, Liam.' (Continue by explaining the reason for the praise.)
2   Achievement – 'Your knees were very straight in your shape.'
3   Challenge – 'Now try to stretch your ankles as well.'

As soon as learners are confident when working in their personal space, have practised locomotion with control and know what is expected of them, they are ready to start travelling around all the spots/mats in the hall, gaining such additional experience as looking where they are going in order to pass by other learners, avoiding collisions and moving into clear spaces.

This, coupled with stopping at vacant spots to make still shapes, progresses their learning, for they now need to concentrate both on the action being performed and also on anticipating the next action. Tasks such as this provide a differentiated learning opportunity for everyone according to individual experience and ability, and also leave the way open for independent learning, personal interpretation and creative movement. Learning to manage locomotion with control lends itself to exploring not only the myriad of ways of travelling on the feet, but also the involvement of the hands with the feet and other parts of the body, such as the seat, front, sides, back, and eventually to taking weight to travel on the hands alone, as in cartwheels and bunny jumps. Exploring the variety of directions, such as forwards, sideways to right and left, backwards and turning, as well as accommodating changes in speeds, including slow, medium and fast, acceleration, deceleration, pause and stop, adds richness to the overall expansion of the movement vocabulary, movement memory and mastery of control.

Building movement vocabulary

The learner's movement vocabulary is made up of the vast myriad of possible movements both that they have already experienced and that which is continually being added through exploration and discovery. For example, here set out in Table 5.1 are ways to explore locomotion:

▨ **Table 5.1** Ways to explore locomotion

On one or both feet

walk	stride	tip toe	march	jog	trot	run

jump along from 2 feet to land on 2 feet

jump along from 2 feet to Right (R) foot	jump along from 2 feet to Left (L) foot
jump along from R foot to 2 feet	jump along from L foot to 2 feet
hop along on R foot	hop along on L foot
leap from L foot to R foot	leap from R foot to L foot

gallop forwards	gallop sideways to the R	gallop sideways to the L
chassee	hopscotch	waltz

skip forwards, backwards and turning

On hands and feet

crawl on hands and knees	walk on hands and feet	run on hands and feet

step on hands and feet with back up	step on hands and feet with back down

step on hands and feet while turning over from back up to front up

step on 2 hands and jump with R foot	step on 2 hands and jump with L foot

climb up	climb down	climb along	climb through

bunny jump along (2 hands and 2 feet)

low cartwheel	medium cartwheel	high cartwheel

On seat, front, side, back

on seat, push backwards with feet	on seat, pull forwards with feet
on front, pull forwards with hands	on front, push backwards with hands
on back, push backwards with feet	on back, pull forwards with feet
roll over in a straight shape	roll over in a tucked shape
roll sideways in a straddle shape	roll sideways in a pike shape

---

Building movement memory and movement quality

In early sessions, learners can readily choose two ways to travel and then change from one to the other to make a sequence. Here, the challenges are to select two that work together, one after the other, and to remember which two ways have been selected, in order to repeat and practise them until they flow smoothly without needing to stop in between. This requires the ability to be performing one action while also anticipating the next and planning how to make a successful change-over. Adding other actions such as a balance increases the challenge further, due not only to the need to commit a third element to memory, but also to the complexity of changing from locomotion to stability. This involves deceleration, stopping and adding a linking action to move into the balance. Movement quality is achieved through working on resilience, control in each element of the sequence, appropriate body awareness and smooth flow between each element. Developing observation, decision-making, communication and self-evaluation skills are invaluable in furthering sequence-building and performance. Peer mentoring (Figure 5.1) enables learners to hone their observation and communication skills. When given a clear focus on what to look for, learners can observe one another in pairs and give supportive and developmental feedback, starting by reporting on what was 'good' and later adding suggestions of what to try to improve next.

■ **Figure 5.1** Peer mentoring

Body awareness

Body awareness can be defined as knowledge of the whole body, particularly focusing on the joints that facilitate movement, including the neck, spine, shoulders, elbows, wrists, hands and the hips, knees, ankles and feet. Body awareness also includes knowledge of the relationship of these joints one to another and the overall shape that results from the wide range of combinations, whether in creating symmetrical or asymmetrical shapes. For example, a *star* shape is seen when the arms and legs are held symmetrically and diagonally away from the spine, with all the joints extended/straight/stretched, whereas in a *tuck* shape, the joints are flexed/bent/folded (Figures 5.2 and 5.3). These shapes can be practised in a variety of positions not only while standing on the feet, but also, for example, in sitting, lying and when upside down. As well as straight, star and tuck, other symmetrical shapes include *straddle* and *pike*. Learners can most easily recognise these when sitting in an 'L' shape, with a straight back and with the legs extended forwards to make a pike shape, and

Arhav

I can make these shapes
on the floor, on a mat, on apparatus

Straight	
Star	
Tuck	

▧ **Figure 5.2** 'I can make these shapes' by Arhav

with the legs spread wide to make straddle, and with extended knees and ankles in both shapes. However, they can also be achieved when standing, on hands and feet, and when lying on the back and even the sides. These are all symmetrical shapes, in which there is no twist in the spine, and learners try to match their arms and their legs.

Afsheen

	I can make these shapes
	on the floor, on a mat, on apparatus
Straight	
Star	
Tuck	

■ **Figure 5.3** 'I can make these shapes' by Afsheen

Exploring asymmetry in making still balances, where the legs and arms do not match each other and where there may be a twist in the spine, leads to the building up of an even more wide-ranging movement vocabulary. Helping learners to focus on named joints, rather than a whole limb, helps to speed up their thinking response time, as they can immediately give attention to the specific body part. For example, learners are often tasked to 'point your toes' when the joints that need to be activated for a successful outcome are the ankles. Tasking learners to 'make straight ankles' gives clear, accurate and succinct information and directive. This helps to avoid any confusion and also obviates the need to translate a verbal instruction into appropriate information to facilitate movement. To achieve a straight leg, learners benefit from guidance to help them to focus on the hips and the knees, as well as the ankles. Starting with the hips and ending with the ankles follows the cephalo-caudal development pattern previously discussed. Similarly, following the proximo-distal development pattern, giving guidance to focus on the shoulders, before the elbows, then the wrists, and finally the fingers, provides learners with useful sequential information when trying to think about straightening the arm. A general maxim is to start from the top and work downwards, and from the centre and work outwards.

Apparatus work (Figures 5.4 and 5.6)

One of the key benefits for learners is the challenge presented by the introduction into the working space of portable and fixed apparatus. These create obstacles to be negotiated and managed, and they add new dimensions, in relation to travelling from the floor onto apparatus, moving while on the apparatus, and from apparatus to the floor. Further experience of travel enables the learner to move from one apparatus set to another. Learners benefit greatly when about half the session is devoted to apparatus work, having been given time to the introduction and floor work phases of the session. Apparatus offers a range of platforms of various heights, such as benches, stools, movement tables and boxes, and

■ **Figure 5.4** Creating shapes on apparatus

surfaces of a range of textures and dimensions, such as ropes, bars and ladders, all of which present a myriad of problems of stability and locomotion to solve through exploration and guided discovery.

For many learners, the apparatus part of each session is much awaited, eagerly anticipated and long remembered. This is the opportunity to develop the learning objective of the session beyond that which the floor has to offer. It is normally considered to be exciting, challenging and fun. For the teacher, the reverse may be the case, especially in the early stages of working with a class of young children in the hall. Learning how to assemble the apparatus, how best to utilise the space and also to maximise the available apparatus is worth establishing well before the first session. The support of a teaching assistant during early sessions is invaluable when working with young children, so that help is available for the children as they learn to work in groups, to move and set up the equipment that they need and then to dismantle and store it after use. Careful planning and organisation can ensure that management routines are established from the start. For example, if the apparatus is stored ready for use around the edges of the hall prior to a session, it only needs to be moved away from the edge and it is ready to use. If needed, to indicate landing areas, or to provide softer landing areas, mats can be added to selected apparatus. Much time is saved when learners are responsible for the setting up of the same set of apparatus for a whole unit, although they usually work with all the apparatus during each session. Once apparatus is set up, the learners can check it for safety, before the teacher or other responsible adult confirms safe assembly and spacing.

Some of the first activities using apparatus are about ways to get onto each piece and ways to get off. Learners can explore for themselves which parts of the body can be

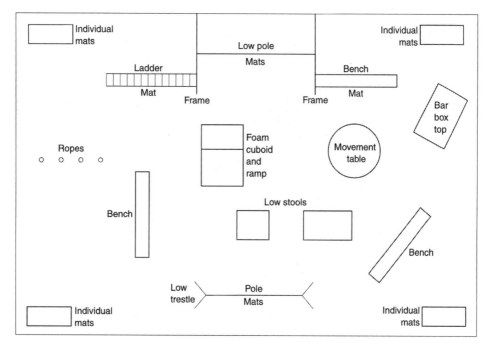

■ **Figure 5.5** Apparatus plan for a unit of work on locomotion and stability

used to get on, including, for example, hands and feet, seat, hip, knees, and front, and which activities can be managed safely, including climbing, stepping, pulling, lifting, turning and twisting. They can also work out appropriate ways to get on forwards, sideways and backwards. Trying this out on all parts of the apparatus that they set up usually precedes locomotion to all other apparatus sets to continue and enhance their experience and enlarge their vocabulary of viable possibilities. Getting off apparatus can follow a similar pattern, though learners need to know that where a mat is provided, it is for use as a landing area from jumps and for other activities such as forward or backward rolls. Choosing where to go next after working on their own apparatus set can normally be determined by individual learner decision as to where there is a free space, rather than in groups or by teacher direction.

For a unit of work in which the focus is on locomotion and stability in extended shape-making. Figure 5.5 illustrates the provision of:

▥ maximum floor area around each piece of apparatus, to allow for many routes to be available for approaching and leaving each set during the travel elements;

▥ low apparatus to enable learners to get on and off each piece easily, so that most attention can be given to practising extended, stable shapes on the apparatus and tidy linking movements between floor and apparatus;

▥ the maximum number of pieces of apparatus with low surfaces for shape-making, so that learners do not have to queue or wait for turns and can concentrate on the quality of their body shape as they work; and

▥ the maximum range of apparatus overall, including fixed apparatus, such as ropes and frames; this will encourage shape-making not only on flat, stable, horizontal surfaces, but also on the less stable surfaces of foam equipment, on slopes and on vertical apparatus such as ropes and frames.

■ **Figure 5.6** 'We are making small, tucked shapes'

Static balance

When finding ways of helping learners to create and hold static balances, the *base* is the parts of the body that are in contact with the floor or apparatus, and upon which the rest of the body is supported. Learning about the parts of the body that make successful bases for static balances and the type of bases that lead to easier and harder balances can help learners to explore ways to widen their vocabulary of balances and build as large a vocabulary as possible for themselves. They can ensure that control is achieved through progressing from easier to harder balances. Categorising balances according to the type of base can provide learners with a clear frame of reference.

The bases suggested below indicate increasing challenge, through progressing from those listed on the left to those on the right. For example, holding a still position on a large base, such as the front, with much of the body in contact with the floor or apparatus, provides greater stability and is therefore easier to hold still than when trying to balance on a small base such as on the ball of one foot. Balancing on two hands and two feet with the back upwards is easier to achieve than balancing on two hands, upside down in a handstand.

Examples of categories of bases that can lead to balances that are easier to achieve or more challenging to achieve are shown in Tables 5.2, 5.3 and 5.4 and Figure 5.7.

■ **Table 5.2** Easier and more challenging bases

Easier bases for static balance	More challenging bases for static balance
Balancing on a large base	Balancing on a small base
Using many parts of the body as the base	Using few parts of the body as the base
Balancing close to the base	Balancing far from the base
Balancing low to the base	Balancing high up, away from the base
Balancing directly over the base	Balancing almost outside the base
Balancing the right way up	Balancing upside down
Balancing on the floor or a mat	Balancing on apparatus

■ **Table 5.3** Examples of bases over which it is normally *easier* to hold static balances

Large base	Many parts as base	The right way up	Body held low on the base	Body held directly over base
Front	Two feet, two hands, head	Sitting	On feet in tuck	On two hands, two feet, back up
Back	Seat, two hands, two feet	Kneeling up	Kneeling low down	Standing on two feet
Side	Two hands, two feet	Standing on back	In tuck	On two hands, two feet, back down

■ **Table 5.4** These bases are normally *more challenging* to use for static balance

Small base	Few body parts as base	Upside-down	Body held high above base	Body leaning outside the base
Hip	One foot	On shoulders	Straight shoulder balance	Two hands, one foot
Foot	Two hands	Headstand	Handstand	On seat, leaning back
Seat	R hand, L foot	Bunny jump	Arabesque	R hand and R foot

■ **Figure 5.7** 'We are finding bases for our balances'

Balances on two feet and two hands with the body in a straight line is a great way to help develop core strength. These balances can be further challenged by turning onto one side in order to balance on one hand and one foot.

Learners can readily understand and use the technical terms for the movement vocabulary that they experience. For example, when balancing on hands and feet, holding the body in straight shapes:

■   front support is the balance on two hands and two feet with the front downwards;
■   back support is the balance on two hands and two feet with the back downwards;

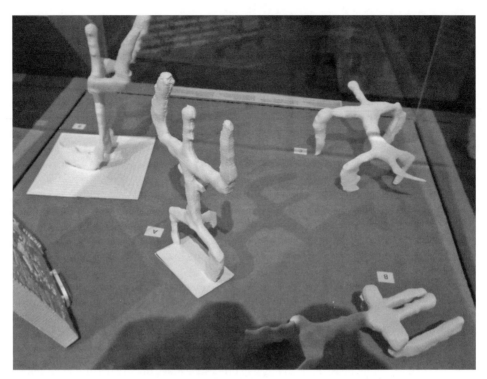

■ **Figure 5.8** Pitoti – a resource for shape-making

www.pitoti.org, by kind permission of Dr Marcel Karnapke, Bauhaus-University Weimar

■ **Figure 5.9** Mirror shapes on apparatus

- side support is a balance on two feet and right hand with the left side upwards;
- side support is a balance on two feet and left hand with the right side upwards; and
- side supports can be further challenged when working on one hand and one foot.

The creative teacher will find many opportunities for developing cross-curricular links with Physical Education. Figures 5.8 and 5.9 show just one example of a stimulus from archaeology, in which learners were discussing archaeological matters using the Pitoti photograph and were encouraged to think about and work on their own shape-making.

Dynamic stability

Dynamic stability involves managing to coordinate and control the body shape while also moving. The potential movement vocabulary to experiment with is unbounded! One example is in *jumping*. Often referred to as 'flight', jumping is the ability to defy gravity, to use muscular strength to project the body weight vertically off the floor or apparatus, into the air, using a powerful drive against the floor or apparatus, through the feet. This is achieved by coordinating the vigorous extension of the ankles, knees and hips from their flexed starting position to project the body upwards, and involves a powerful forward and upward swing of the arms to add lift to the jump. While control in the 'take-off' phase is fundamental to the success of the jump, equally important are the coordination of the body to sustain control while airborne, and body tension, core stability, resilience and balance in landing. The challenges for the teacher are to develop all three phases of the jump (the take-off, flight phase and landing), in order to achieve quality performance and to facilitate exploration of the extensive range of vocabulary of jumps.

Here are some ideas to explore when experimenting with jumping and landing:

- Jump from two feet to land on two feet on the spot, forwards, backwards, sideways and turning to Right (R) and Left (L).
- Hop on R foot and L foot on the spot, forwards, backwards, sideways and turning to R and L.
- Jump from two feet to L foot and two feet to R foot.
- Jump from R foot to two feet and jump from L foot to two feet.
- Hopscotch – continuous sequence of jumping from one foot to land on two feet, taking off from two feet to land on the other foot.
- Leap – from R to L foot and from L to R foot.
- Take-off action for approaching apparatus (step and take off from one foot to land on two feet and immediately jump from two feet to land on apparatus on two feet).
- Jump down from apparatus to land on two feet.
- Jump up onto apparatus, using hands to assist and without hand assistance.

Another example of dynamic stability is *rolling*.

Rolling is the continuous, smooth and successive transfer of body weight from one surface to the next adjacent surface, while protecting the joints and bony surfaces from knocking against the floor or apparatus. Complete rolls should go through 360 degrees, and should be continuous, resilient and silent, as well as showing clarity of body shape throughout. There are two main axes of rotation for rolling in gymnastics. These are the longitudinal axis, for sideways rolling, and the horizontal axis, for rolling forwards and backwards. For most children aged 4–7 years, the main focus is normally on sideways rolling.

The longitudinal axis

Imagine a pin that goes in through the feet and comes out through the head, rather like roasting a pig on a spit! Rolling sideways is the technique to be explored around this axis. Learners can usually roll sideways, to the right and left, but many are not able to achieve this successfully with a straight body shape, with the elbows, wrists and fingers extended above the head, with the arms shoulder-width apart, and with the hips, knees and ankles extended and held together. Learners who lack core stability find it difficult to maintain the upper and lower halves of the body in a straight line, and others who lack body awareness find it difficult to manage the control of the arms and legs, because they cannot see the limbs during the rolling action and must rely on kinaesthetic awareness, or the 'feel' of the position of their limbs.

Further detail can be seen in Maude (2003).

Learners can explore other ways for rolling around the longitudinal axis by altering their body shape. For example, by making a small, flexed, tucked shape, they can roll from the knees to the side, to the back and onto the knees, by carefully tucking in their elbows and keeping the eyes open to check for clear spaces to roll into. Learners with good core strength could also try the 'dish' shape, starting from lying on the back with the legs and arms held off the floor or rolling surface, making a curved or crescent shape and then rolling with only the pelvis in contact with the floor. Additionally, from a starting shape, sitting in a straddle, with wide legs and extended knees and ankles, learners can hold onto their legs, lean to one side and lower down to roll from that side, over the back to the other side ands then sit up again in straddle.

Table 5.5 provides some suggestions for building a vocabulary of rolls around the longitudinal axis, categorised according to body shape, direction of travel, and start and end positions.

■ **Table 5.5** Rolling using the longitudinal axis

Body shape	Extended on whole body
	Extended in dish shape, on pelvis
	Tucked, starting and ending on knees
	Straddle from seat, with wide legs
	Alternate flexion and extension of knees during roll, from a kneeling start on one knee
Direction	Sideways to the right
	Sideways to the left
Start and end positions	On back
	On front
	On knees
	On seat
	On one knee and the other foot

To increase the movement vocabulary and to add to the challenge and complexity of the work, learners can roll not only on the floor, but can also roll along apparatus, such as a padded box top, and from inclined apparatus, such as a matted springboard or a foam ramp, onto a mat. Changing body shape and extension and flexion of arms and legs during rolls provides additional challenge to coordination and control. Similar or contrasting rolls can be joined into sequences or can be built into sequences with other actions on floor and apparatus.

Dynamic stability can also be experienced, for example, when:

■ moving into and out of stable positions, linking actions on floor and apparatus;
■ travelling on the floor and apparatus;
■ jumping on the floor, onto and from apparatus with turns on feet, in jumps, in rolls, when circling on a horizontal pole or between ropes;
■ twisting at the waist on floor, on apparatus and from apparatus;
■ spinning on seat or foot;
■ swinging from the hands on a horizontal pole or rope or from the backs of the knees on a pole;
■ climbing on frame, ladder or rope; and
■ inverting in bunny jump, low cartwheel or handstand on a mat and when swinging on ropes.

A unit of work can very usefully be built around a theme such as 'exploring my ankles and knees', in which the learning is focused on gaining awareness and knowledge of extension and flexion of the knees and ankles in achieving efficient function, fluency

Working with my knees and ankles			
	Very good work	Good work	Needs practice
Straight knees			
Straight ankles			
Straight knees and ankles			

■ **Figure 5.10** Bee's chart of ankle and knee work

Working with my knees and ankles			
	Very good work	**Good work**	**Needs practice**
Straight knees	Pike	roundoff	bridge
Straight ankles	Straddle	hand Stand	cart wheel
Straight knees and ankles	Shoulder Stand	Press up.	splits.

■ **Figure 5.11** Matt's chart of ankle and knee work

and artistry in performance. When learners can see their knees and ankles, they can more readily evaluate and give feedback on their learning, whereas this is much more difficult when these are not visible.

Bee (aged 5, Figure 5.10) and Matt (aged 7, Figure 5.11) used their classroom-based follow-up session to draw their learning evaluations. Evaluations such as these not only provide useful assessment evidence of learners' own understanding, but also enable the teacher to target future learning opportunities.

SUMMARY

In this chapter, we have considered ways in which learners can develop their physical competence, knowledge and understanding of movement through experiencing movement vocabulary, movement memory and movement quality in *locomotion* and *stability*, in the context of gymnastic activities. Valuing opportunities for exploration and meaning-making is motivating, and relates to our POWER principles as *purposeful*, as this enables learners to make meaningful connections, learning how to evaluate the conditions for achieving control, coordination, body and spatial awareness on floor and apparatus. *Opportunities* that draw on children's interests, that are age/stage appropriate and that make the most of opportunities in and across the curriculum can provide learners time and support to be creative, adventurous and independent learners where they develop an awareness of their bodies in space. This is best achieved by teachers with sound subject knowledge, mindful of children's *well-being*. Practitioners who provide a 'can-do' environment, whose teaching styles encourage learning through guided discovery, who, through creative teaching, offer appropriate levels of challenge, who give developmental feedback and devise opportunities for learners to succeed with confidence and enable them *enthusiastically* to try out activities and extend their learning horizons.

FURTHER READING

Bailey, R. and Macfadyen, T. (2000) *Teaching Physical Education 5–11*, London: Continuum.

Benn, B., Benn, T. and Maude, P. (2007) *A Practical Guide to Teaching Gymnastics*, Leeds: Coachwise.

British Gymnastics (2013) *Schemes and Awards*, available at: www.british-gymnastics.co.uk (accessed 1 January 2014).

British Heart Foundation (2013) *Early Movers*, Loughborough: British Heart Foundation.

Hopper, B., Grey, J. and Maude, P. (2000) *Teaching Physical Education in the Primary School*, London: Routeldge.

Lavin, J. (ed.) (2008) *Creative Approaches to Physical Education: Helping Children to Achieve Their True Potential*, Abingdon: Routledge.

Maude, P. (2003) *Observing Children Moving*, CD-ROM, Reading: afPE and Tacklesport.

Visual Learning Company (2007) *Gymnastics*, DVD, www.visuallearning.co.uk.

Youth Sport Trust (2012) *Start to Move*, Loughborough: Youth Sport Trust, available at: www.youthsporttrust.org (accessed 1 January 2014).

CHAPTER 6

DEVELOPING GYMNASTICS

INTRODUCTION

In 350 BC, Aristotle stated: 'The principle of gymnastics is the education of all youth and not simply the minority of people favoured by nature'. With this in mind and building on Chapter 5, the content of this chapter is designed to enable the creative teacher to offer all children aged 7–11 years a gymnastics learning experience that is accessible, challenging and fit for purpose. The purposes are, first, for all learners to expand their movement knowledge, understanding and performance standards in order that they can transfer their gymnastics-related learning to their general lifelong movement competence and future experience. The second purpose is that learners, for whom gymnastics holds the potential for further pursuit, will have laid a sound foundation for their future progress.

In addition to the traditional forms of gymnastics, learners may aspire to become participants in other popular activities, such as street gymnastics, parkour and free running. These sports require skilful and efficient movement, in unconventional environments. They are readily accessible to those who can jump, land, roll, vault, leap and climb, and who are resilient, able to manage their body weight quickly, use momentum, and absorb and redistribute energy as they travel from obstacle to obstacle in the environment. Facing and managing risk, maintaining safe practice and enjoying the seemingly impossible challenges presented by the environment offer endless enjoyment for experts in these gymnastic-type activities. Others may aspire to become circus acrobats, stunt performers or to join companies such as Cirque du Soleil, and achieve the fantastic feats of physical virtuosity and performance confidence. Examples of other sports that incorporate elements of gymnastics include diving, synchronised swimming, skateboarding, BMX cycling and rock climbing.

Most children will be proceeding well on their physical literacy journey by the time they reach Key Stage 2, aged 7 years, and will be able to use their school-based gymnastics experiences to enhance this further through increased knowledge and physical competence. For some, they will be able to find new levels of motivation and confidence in what they can do. Opportunities to select appropriately daring and safe challenges, to persist even when not always successful, to maintain a positive attitude to learning, and to build on their determination to succeed are qualities to explore in Key Stage 2. These qualities can also increase learners' knowledge, understanding and experience of ways of maintaining and increasing their physical fitness. Gymnastic activities call for strength, flexibility and stamina. For example, muscular strength in the upper body is enhanced when climbing, hanging and swinging, and when jumping or taking weight on hands in partner work or in bunny jumps, cartwheels and handstands. Stamina is challenged when engaging in sustained physical activity and when working at speed (e.g. in cardio-respiratory activity, such as getting out of breath). Flexibility is experienced through opening of active joints to their maximum extension, through careful management of the muscles, ligaments and tendons around those joints, to increase and control maximum range of movement.

Creative ways of developing gymnastics at Key Stage 2, then, as with all the areas of physical activity that we discuss in this book, are based on the development of secure and confident subject knowledge and an understanding of the potential teachers have to bring to the learner body confidence and power. At Key Stage 2, we are concerned with the ways that learners are able to make connections within and through their learning, draw on previous knowledge, skills and understanding in order to build new learning, and, in doing so, gaining greater understanding of their bodies. This is *purposeful* and engages learners in *opportunities* for meaning-making. Such meaning-making is motivating and aids *well-being*, as it enables learners to gain positive experiences from Physical Education. However, learners will thrive best in an *environment* that provides appropriate material or content and carefully considers the role(s) of the learners according to their age, stage, abilities and interests. At Key Stage 2, learners can indeed be fully involved in evaluating and improving their performance and *revelling* in their improvements and successes.

KEY ASPECTS

Learners from the age of about 7 years have emerged from their early years of rapid growth and have not yet embarked on the physical changes that occur at puberty. These are the 'skill-hungry' years, when, with relative stability in growth and with the movement patterns of locomotion, stability and object control already established and practised in their previous

■ **Figure 6.1** Balance on hands in tuck (also called 'kettle stand')

■ **Figure 6.2** Year 6 creating partner work in a unit on levels in gymnastics

school curriculum, learners are more readily in a position to explore more creative and demanding experiences such as can be seen in Figure 6.1. Gymnastics is able to offer many of these, both within and beyond the school curriculum. Some learners may be eager to devise and work through progressions for named gymnastics agilities, such as forward and backward roll, cartwheel and handstand (for progressive activities, see Benn *et al.* 2007), and everyone will be able to apply their previous learning of gymnastic activities in a variety of creative ways.

The currently accepted traditional 'disciplines' of gymnastics include: men's and women's artistic gymnastics, tumbling, acrobatic gymnastics, rhythmic gymnastics, aerobic gymnastics, team gymnastics, display gymnastics, gymfusion, trampolining and cheerleading, as found in the British Gymnastics Resources. Within artistic gymnastics, the key activities are work on the floor and mats, horizontal, parallel and asymmetric bars, on beam, vault, rings and pommels. The most suitable equivalent apparatus for primary schools includes floor and mat work, benches instead of beam, stools, movement tables and boxes for vaulting activities, and poles attached to fixed apparatus for bar work. Rhythmic gymnastics includes rope, hoop, ribbon, ball and clubs. In primary school, the equivalent activity is manipulative gymnastics, and includes a range of ropes of varying lengths, several sizes of hoops, short ribbons, and balls that bounce well. Together, these offer ideal opportunities for exploring and gaining increased experience of manipulative gymnastics. In acrobatic gymnastics, balance and cooperation are the keys to success, in order to create and share balances and linked sequences with others.

In artistic and manipulative gymnastics, learners can investigate the movement qualities of each piece of apparatus and, in all three forms, can devise compositions alone, in pairs and in groups. Individual activities can be developed to enhance movement performance, knowledge and understanding, and increase learners' vocabulary of gymnastic actions through analysing what they can already do and then extending their experience. They can also expand their insights through observing other learners and through giving focused feedback, thereby enhancing their observation, analysis, communication and social skills, as well as internalising achievements to incorporate into their own work. The three forms of artistic, rhythmic and acrobatic gymnastics will be discussed in this chapter, with a focus on artistic gymnastics in the first two years and on acrobatic and manipulative gymnastics in the latter two years.

Learners normally come into Key Stage 2 with a rich movement vocabulary that was enhanced through the school curriculum and built upon active outdoor play in the early years. They should be familiar with the organisation of gymnastics sessions, with the preparation session (often called 'warm up'), with floor work and the subsequent apparatus work, and the summative evaluation and ending of sessions. They should be accustomed to the partner and group work necessary for successful apparatus handling, lifting, carrying, spacing, placing, setting up and safety checking, as well as dismantling and putting everything away. They should be well able to transfer their knowledge from Key Stage 1 in order to learn the handling of apparatus, which is reserved for use in Key Stage 2 and is therefore new to them. In Key Stage 2, learners will continue to explore ways to extend their gymnastics movement vocabulary, increase their movement memory and enhance their movement quality. They will also increasingly be able to draw on other movement forms that can appropriately be applied to gymnastics, such as bouncing, throwing and catching a ball from games activities, or ways of travelling, turning and jumping from dance.

One of the roles of the teacher is to challenge children to explore and develop *dimensions of movement* (Figure 6.3) in their learning, such as those related to body shape, directions, speeds, rhythms, pathways, levels, and partner and group work, and to apply these when working on floor, mats and with apparatus.

Scenario

Another of the teacher's roles is to enable learners to analyse their own performance in order to improve movement quality. Some of the qualities of movement that children in Key Stage 2 can enhance include coordination, control, poise, maximum efficiency, minimum effort, minimum outlay of time and energy, resilience, stamina, flexibility, strength, and body and spatial awareness. Could your learners create their own chart to record their learning and achievement in these qualities of movement?

Creating sequences

In addition to increasing their movement vocabulary, learners will be able to extend their movement memory through researching, selecting, creating and building increasingly complex sequences of gymnastic movement. Increasingly complex sequences will contain both a greater number of actions and links, but also greater challenge with regard to *movement dimensions*. Figure 6.4 is an example of a chart, marked out as a grid that is

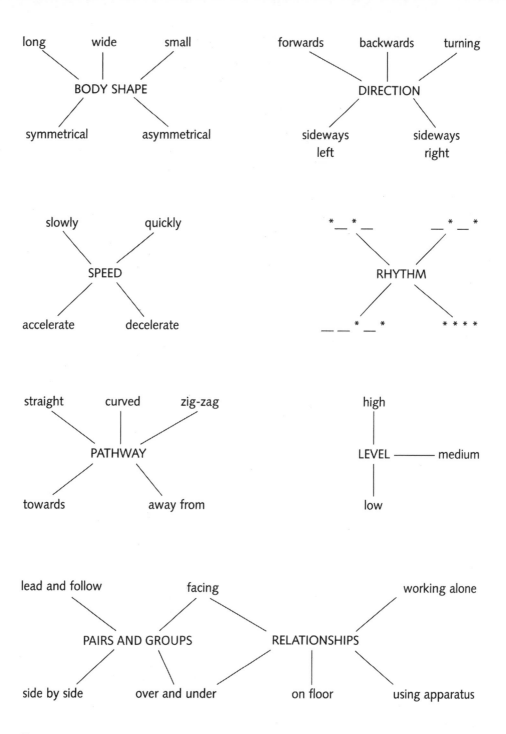

Key:
* short beat
— long beat

Figure 6.3 Movement dimensions to aid the development of movement quality through gymnastics

	Travel on feet	Travel on hands and feet	Jump and land	Roll	Balance	Turn	Pull	Push	Hang	Swing	Climb
Extended long			**F2**								
Extended wide			**1**								
Flexed											
Symmetry						**Ii**					
Asymmetry											
Forwards											
Backwards			**F6**								
Sideways left	**a ii**										
Sideways right				**4**							
Straight							**a iii**				
Curved											
Zig-zag											
High/up					**3**						**A3**
Medium											
Low/down						**I ii**					**A5**
Slowly											
Quickly	**F1**										
Accelerating											
Decelerating											
Pause					**I iii**				**A4**		
Rhythm											
Right way up											
Upside-down		**2**			**a i**						

■ **Figure 6.4** Chart for creating gymnastic sequences and developing movement memory designed to serve as a self-guiding tool for learners to explore and draw from, and with which they can experiment, select, record and evaluate their selected sequences. This grid could also be used as a means for them to audit their achievements.

The chart (Figure 6.4) is made up of gymnastics actions, which are shown in the grid on the horizontal axis, such as travel on hands and feet, roll and climb. In the grid on the vertical axis are selected elements of the movement dimension. Cells within the grid can be labelled to indicate the combination of action and dimension that have been selected in any one sequence. One of the factors that can lead to early success is when learners create short sequences that can be repeated and refined until they can be performed with accuracy, poise and minimum effort. Three sequences are shown, with the first in grey cells labelled 1, 2, 3, 4. The second is in grey-shaded boxes with lower-case letters, and the third sequence is shown in white cells with upper-case letters.

In one example, the learner chose to make a sequence of four actions. The example is shown in grey on the grid:

1   Jump and land, showing a wide extended shape in the air.
2   Travel on hands and feet in an upside down position.
3   Balance high up.
4   Roll, sideways to the right.

When learners use the floor and the apparatus in sequences, they have additional considerations to determine, such as how they will approach, access, use and leave the selected apparatus. In this sequence, the learner used F for floor work and A for work on apparatus. The sequence below shows the decisions that the learner made:

F1   Travel on feet quickly.
F2   Jump with extension to apparatus.
A3   Climb up high.
A4   Hang and pause.
A5   Climb down.
F6   Roll backwards.

Within each of the headings, there is also a multiplicity of options that could be selected in performing that action in addition to applying *movement dimensions* (Figure 6.3). For example, the movement vocabulary for jumping includes the list in Table 6.1 below. Jumping can be on the spot, travelling forwards, backwards, sideways to right and left, and turning to right and left. Jumping can also involve taking weight on hands in a tucked shape known as bunny jump, cartwheel with flight or somersault.

■ **Table 6.1** Creating movement vocabulary for jumping

From two feet to two feet	From two feet to right foot	From two feet to left foot
From left foot to two feet	From right foot to two feet	From right foot to left foot
From left foot to right foot	From right foot to right foot	From left foot to left foot

Linking

For every pair of actions, there will normally be a linking movement to join the two, in order to achieve a continuous piece of gymnastics. Linking movements have a whole vocabulary of their own, and need focused teaching and learning opportunities within units and sessions. In the example in Figure 6.4, the learner, who was focusing on links between actions, recorded actions as 'a' and links as 'l':

a i   Balance upside down.
l i   Turn with symmetry.
a ii   Travel on feet, sideways to the left.
l ii   Turn, low down.
a iii Pull straight.
l iii Balance and pause.

Although many gymnastics skills are symmetrical, asymmetry, such as the use of twisting, can readily be explored to create linking actions.

Here are some examples of symmetrical and asymmetrical links when returning to standing from a shoulder balance. Learners could try:

▓ rolling down the spine to back lie, flexing arms and legs into a tucked shape and sideways rolling onto knees and stepping forwards to transfer weight onto one foot after the other to stand;

▓ rolling down the spine to back lie, sideways rolling to front lie, pushing up to front support and jumping from front support to feet to stand;

▓ rolling down the spine, placing the feet on the mat near the seat and reaching forward with the hands to come onto the feet to stand up;

▓ continuing the backward momentum, to roll over one shoulder onto the knees, by twisting at the waist and pushing with hands flat on floor beside ear, from the knees step up to stand; and

▓ continuing the backward momentums with a twist, to roll over one shoulder onto the front, using the hands for control and to protect the neck, then push up to front support and jump the feet under the hips to stand.

For example, having landed onto two feet from a jump and linking into a sideways extended roll, the learner could:

▓ lower into a tuck position and place the hands on the mat behind to sit down, lie down and finally extend the hips, knees and ankles and the shoulders, elbows and wrists, ready to roll;

▓ reach forward, place the hands and forward roll to back lie; and

▓ twist and lower into side-sitting and extend the whole body while moving onto the back or front.

These are just a few suggestions. Giving learners opportunities for exploring and perfecting the multiplicity of links between any two actions can lead to some of the most creative and attractive compositions of gymnastic movement.

Use of apparatus

In units of work based on floor and apparatus, at least half of each session should be allocated to apparatus work. Learners can then extend their floor-based experience, explore and capitalise on the properties of the apparatus resources available, and gain experience of working safely in a more demanding environment. Many learners consider that the apparatus constitutes a more exciting and challenging environment than the floor. There is much to explore at various heights, on a variety of surfaces, of different textures and dimensions, as well as on single pieces and combinations of apparatus. Learners can find and perfect ways to approach and leave apparatus, to get on and off apparatus, to move while on apparatus, and create sequences alone, in pairs and in groups. They need time to incorporate skills and sequence elements learnt on the floor into their apparatus work, as well as to develop specific skills that can only be perfected through the use of apparatus. Creating their own apparatus sets provides further challenges to new learning. Bars, ropes and other fixed apparatus demand upper-body strength, whereas tables, benches, boxes and stools used for jumping and landing demand leg strength and postural control. Core body strength is needed to achieve balance positions that are partly on apparatus and partly on the floor or a mat. Perfecting postural stability and balance can be achieved on every piece of apparatus, as can a wide range of skills of locomotion when approaching, accessing, working on and leaving apparatus. Creating continuous, flowing sequences, including work on two or three apparatus sets, with a variety of locomotion skills on feet, hands and feet, and other parts of the body in order to travel from one apparatus set to the next offers

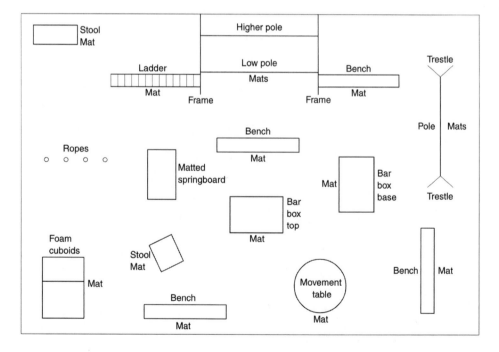

■ **Figure 6.5** Apparatus plan

demanding challenges to even the most competent gymnast! See Figure 6.5 for a suggested apparatus plan. The creative teacher encourages learners to work and succeed at their own level, and to expand their performance and achievement boundaries. A useful theme for a unit of work designed to enable learners to maximise their apparatus experience is 'Levels'.

Learners might start by focusing on their footwork and produce sequences in which the feet are demonstrably at low, medium and high levels, such as in Figures 6.6 and 6.7. For example, locomotion in the form of step patterns and travelling actions can be contrasted

■ **Figure 6.6** High level

with inversion activities, elevating the feet above the rest of the body as in tucked and extended shoulder stands, low and extended headstands, bunny jumps, and low and full cartwheels on the floor or on mats. However, once learners transfer work to apparatus, they can access a far greater range of movement vocabulary, and can focus on work at low, medium and high levels in climbing, hanging, swinging and working upside down. They can find links to transfer from level to level. In pairs, they can work at contrasting levels, as in the photograph of Year 6 learners earlier in this chapter (Figure 6.2) and here, as a group (Figure 6.8).

■ **Figure 6.7** Medium level

■ **Figure 6.8** Group work – feet highest

Two other forms of gymnastics are well suited to learners in Key Stage 2, namely *acrobatic* gymnastics and *manipulative* gymnastics. Acrobatic gymnastics is as much about learning to cooperate in pairs and groups in planning and creating, remembering, recalling and performing agreed sequences as it is about the ability to perform complex acrobatic skills and activities. Acrobatic gymnastics can be the most rewarding experience in Physical Education for many learners. One learner who had not previously enjoyed any gymnastics work in primary school evaluated her acrobatic gymnastics unit in Year 8 as follows:

> I really enjoyed this unit. It's really boosted my confidence. I've enjoyed working with different groups of people. I've been able to teach other people things they didn't know before and that's really good.
>
> (Benn *et al.* 2007)

What can creative teaching of acrobatic gymnastics offer?

Learners can draw from their past experience of working with others, though now the challenge is to cooperate in a variety of specifically challenging ways. As a means of staging progression for the learners, activities might fall into the following categories.

Non-contact pairs gymnastics

1   Mirroring one another, performing the same skills and links, while facing each other and aiming to appear in unison throughout.

2   Matching by working side by side.
3   Matching by leading and following.
4   Matching by moving towards and away from each other.
5   Contrasting one another with one learner in a stable high position and the partner travelling under him or her, or with one learner low down and the partner going over him or her (working over the feet of the learner, rather than the head).
6   Producing sequences containing a variety of these.
7   Peer mentoring through observation, analysis and feedback to partner.

Contact pairs gymnastics

An added challenge in partner work is for learners to achieve and include balances that are in controlled contact with one another. For example, in balances on one foot, such as the arabesque, learners can place one hand on the partner's shoulder, or in sitting with legs extended and raised up, the sole of the foot could be in contact.

Activities such as these are often practised before introducing counterbalance, which has its own implications for careful management by both partners, since both partners shift their weight from over the base to outside the base and depend on their partner to prevent falling and to ensure a safe exit for them both. This can be explored using low apparatus at first, with one partner sitting on the apparatus in a strong and stable position and the other standing facing him or her. Each partner holds just above the wrists of their partner and the sitting partner leans back gently and returns. After both partners are familiar with this activity, they can try again, but with the standing partner also leaning away and returning. These progressions help to ensure a full understanding of safe counterbalancing before practising with both partners standing.

Partial weight-taking pairs gymnastics

In primary school curriculum gymnastics, it is realistic to confine work to partial weight-taking and for full weight-taking balances to be confined to extracurricular activity, with a specifically qualified teacher. Before working with a partner, learners can use apparatus such as low boxes, benches, padded box top, and stools to practise not only a range of balances, but also to find ways of moving into balances and ways of leaving them. Apparatus work in which part of the body is on the apparatus and part on the mat helps both to enhance core stability and control, with straight body lines and correct shoulder and hip angles, and enables learners to self-check and peer-check the positions prior to replacing the apparatus with a partner. Learners should also self-check and peer-check the stability and control of their balance positions when working as base, and practise ways to move into and out of the base balance.

Key learning opportunities in partial and total weight-bearing activities with a partner involve discovering and mastering ways to work both as the 'base' partner and as the 'top' partner. An important discussion and decision would be about which of the pair would make the stronger, more stable base and which the lighter top. Learners must also consider the responsibilities of taking on each of these roles, including how to ensure the safety of both members of the partnership at all times. Learners usually start by working alone, to practise control in the balance positions of both base and top, so that they can begin to appreciate the role of each partner and build an appropriate movement vocabulary. They will also work on finding and fine-tuning ways to move towards and into their selected balance positions and ways of carefully leaving again, so that the base is comfortable throughout. Working alongside their partner also facilitates communication and peer mentoring in order to share the outcomes of both practising alone and to arrive at mutual decisions about how best to proceed and succeed as a pair. Guided discovery with the teacher can help to ensure that learners appreciate the parameters of their work together and are realistic in their expectations of each other!

One of the most stable bases for partial weight-taking is on hands and knees, with the shoulders above the hands and the hips above the knees, thereby creating a square shape with strong right angles. Another is supported sitting in tuck and also in the sitting position in straddle, so that the widely spread legs add stability and also enable the top to approach from in front as in Figure 6.9.

The balance for the hands and knees base is a square shape with the shoulders above the hands and the hips above the knees, and the position of support for the top is with the hands on the strong bony pelvis and hip area of the base. Approaching from the side usually precedes approaching over the feet. Placing the hands into front support on the base usually precedes placing the feet, and the top in front support usually precedes back support. In the tucked-base balance, the base sits with bent knees, with feet flat on the mat and with the hands flat on the mat for support and behind and near the hips. The top can now place the hands on the knees of the base in a front support or back support balance. The straddle sit makes a wide and stable base. The top might start from behind the base by placing the hands on the shoulders of the base, as this offers a clear point from which to

■ **Figure 6.9** Pairs balances

access and leave the balance. The wide straddle shape is also useful when approaching from in front, as it provides a clear access space for the top when placing the fronts of the feet on the shoulders of the base.

Giving learners encouragement to seek out their own workable ways to make bases and balances that are capable of partial weight-bearing can produce amazing results in cooperative learning, with everyone working according to their ability and experience, and with empathy and motivation towards a finished product. As they work on creating sequences of paired work, learners can also use their ingenuity and skill to find ways for the base and the top to access and leave balances, and for both partners to add locomotion, jumps and other skills to their sequences.

Manipulative gymnastics

Although the two categories of locomotion and stability feature more strongly in gymnastic activities, the third category, namely manipulative learning, can also readily be developed within the primary school gymnastics curriculum. Manipulative activities are related to rhythmic gymnastics, and offer wide-ranging learning opportunities through working with ropes, balls, hoops and ribbons. Although the traditional discipline of rhythmic gymnastics is restricted to females, learners in primary school, both boys and girls, can be offered successful learning opportunities for creative and skilful movement, through experimenting with, manipulating and controlling each piece of apparatus, and through extending their movement vocabulary, movement memory and movement quality. Additionally, whereas

■ **Figure 6.10** Manipulative gymnastics

not all children relish the opportunities for adventure when presented, for example, with an obstacle such as a movement table or set of climbing ropes, they may greatly benefit from, enjoy and be more adventurous in trying out ideas for themselves when working with manipulative apparatus. In Figure 6.10 learners work with ball, rope, hoop and ribbon.

Scenario

Learners worked in four groups, with ropes in one area, ribbons in another, balls in a third and hoops in the fourth area. They were tasked to explore the particular qualities of their piece of apparatus, while keeping it near to them and working on the spot first, in their own personal space. To stimulate extension of movement vocabulary and promote peer mentoring, the learners also worked as a group to find as many activities as they could think of. Learners took turns to show one idea for everyone in the group to try, so that each learner had opportunities to contribute and demonstrate, and the score of activities was kept. The groups rotated from one apparatus type to the next, accumulating as many activities as they could. This provided a rich platform for subsequent selection of content for sequence creation.

Teaching points might be to praise learners who manage to control the apparatus, offer appropriate activities for their peers to try, and accumulate a high score of *movement vocabulary* ideas.

In progressing from working on the spot, in their personal space, learners might add a variety of jumps or add travelling in the general space, while still keeping the apparatus under control and near to them.

To develop *movement memory*, learners could then be tasked to select three/four/five or more activities to put into a continuous, repeatable sequence, perhaps alternating an activity on the spot with an activity that travels. Peer observation and feedback helps to ensure that repetition is of the same sequence, helping his or her partner to practise until the sequence is the best it can be, to the learner's satisfaction.

The three main challenges presented in developing *movement quality* in manipulative gymnastics are:

1   to keep the apparatus moving, so that an observer can trace a continuous, progressive path;
2   to maintain the apparatus under control at all times; and
3   to work with the apparatus at maximum amplitude in relation to the learner, so that when fully competent, the learner works from extended posture, on the balls of the feet, rather than on flat feet, and the apparatus becomes an extension of the already extended limb (e.g. when using a ribbon, maintain an extended elbow, so that the ribbon stick and ribbon are as far away as possible from the body).

Feedback to a learner by a peer mentor, on these points, as well as on the originality of work shown, can not only support the learner, but also provide valuable feedback from observation to the mentor.

Table 6.2 Building movement vocabulary in manipulative gymnastics

Some examples of movement vocabulary in manipulative gymnastics

Elements	Ball	Hoop	Ribbon	Rope
Standing still	Roll around body, send up bounce and catch	Circle around waist ('hula-hoop'), skip	Small to large ripples on floor, ribbon in right and left hand	Circle rope at sides, skip forwards and backward
Travelling forwards	Roll along floor, run past ball, turn and collect	Roll along with right and left hand	Snake at one side and the other	Skip along, walking, jumping, running
Travelling sideways to right and to left	Pass from hand to hand	Circle around wrist, waist, foot	Ripple, swish, circle in front	Swing, circle, skip forwards and backwards
Travelling backwards	Roll along arms	Roll hoop away with spin, so that it comes back	Circle in front, at sides, above head	Circle above head
Turning	Bounce and catch	Place hoop over head to floor and up again	Wave ribbon up and down quickly	Skip backwards on the spot
Apparatus on the floor/ in the air	Send up high, allow to bounce and catch	Transfer from hand to hand, high up, low down	Make figure of 8 from medium to high to low	Hold folded rope high and low in both hands
Apparatus far from the body (extend) and keep apparatus moving	Throw ball up, let bounce and then catch	Keep hoop moving, near to and far from body, to sides	Run, leap with ribbon circling and straight arm	Fold rope, toss up, catch ends and skip
Balance with apparatus	Extended shapes, ball on hand	One leg balance with hoop on other foot	Balance and draw your name with the ribbon	Arabesque, with circling rope
Jump and land with apparatus	Throw up, jump to catch	Roll, step, leap, collect	Run, leap, circle ribbon high up	Skip doubles and cross arm skip
Create a sequence	Own choice (e.g. bounce, roll, throw up, catch, travel, jump, balance)	Own choice (e.g. circle, roll, spin, catch, go through, travel, leap)	Own choice (e.g. circle, wave, ripple, swish, travel, jump, roll)	Own choice (e.g. circle, swing, skip, toss and catch, travel, jump)

Building movement vocabulary in manipulative gymnastics

Some ideas for developing a bank of movement vocabulary with each piece of equipment is shown in Table 6.2, but this is in no way intended to be a 'straitjacket' to restrict the creativity and fun of finding out what the apparatus can do. Each piece of apparatus has its own special properties, as well as generalised activities, to master. Indeed, learners could create their own chart to record the vocabulary that they have found and can do. Future challenges and skills that they are 'working towards' and aspiring to achieve could also be indicated (Benn *et al.* 2007).

Once learners are competent and confident in their own ability and can compose and perform solo sequences with ball, ribbon, hoop and rope, the time has come to work with another learner and set about expanding their knowledge and competence. Exchanging apparatus with a partner, matching, mirroring, leading, and following and creating floor and air patterns leads onto selecting activities to include in performance routines. By the end of the primary school years (age 11), learners are well able to work with several others and create group sequences such that a unit of work in manipulative gymnastics may culminate in group work that is practised, repeated, completed and ready to present to an audience.

SUMMARY

Consider, from your creative teaching, what your learners will achieve and take with them from their primary school gymnastics experience, into their secondary school education, their extracurricular activities and on into the rest of their lives, in terms of skilful and creative gymnastics achievements, physical competence and all other aspects of physical literacy.

FURTHER READING

Benn, B., Benn, T. and Maude, P. (2007) *A Practical Guide to Teaching Gymnastics*, Leeds: Coachwise.

British Gymnastics (2013) *Schemes and Awards*, available at: www.british-gymnastics.org (accessed 1 January 2014).

Maude, P. and Whitehead, M. (2004) *Observing and Analysing Learners' Movement*, CD-ROM, Reading: afPE and Tacklesport.

CHAPTER 7

INTRODUCING GAMES ACTIVITIES

INTRODUCTION

This chapter is about creative teaching and learning through the curriculum of games activities for children aged between 4 and 7 years. It is only in school that every child, regardless of ability and prior experience, is entitled to high-quality Physical Education that inspires all pupils to succeed, excel and lead healthy, active lives. This chapter is to enable teachers to extend children's physical literacy through the provision of stimulating and challenging games activities. Essential to the development of physical literacy is the building of movement competence, movement vocabulary, movement memory and movement quality, and knowledge and understanding, while also enhancing the motivation and confidence of all learners. A further capacity is the development of imagination and curiosity, and the embedding of creative intelligence. The Early Years and Key Stage 1 are important for laying the foundation for lifelong participation in physical activity.

Robinson (2001: 137) states that intelligence is essentially creative, and that our lives are 'shaped by the ideas we use to give them meaning'. Nurturing children's ability to generate ideas that can be explored through movement is an invaluable means of enhancing creative intelligence, particularly for those who readily find kinaesthetic learning to be the most accessible. Robinson (2001: 137) also reminds us that 'creativity is possible in all areas of human activity', and that 'it draws from intuitions and feelings as well as from practical knowledge and skills', involving a process of 'seeing new possibilities'. In relation to games activities, this suggests that through active participation, children can acquire practical knowledge and a wide range of physical skills, which can build up their understanding and physical competence, their refined movement patterns, coordination and control, as they become mature movers. To these abilities can be added the nurturing of cognitive, social and emotional development through games playing, whereby children gain experience of important life skills, such as cooperation, empathy, responsibility, decision-making, fair play, competition, tactics, safe risk-taking, and losing as well as winning. Through acquiring understanding of the elements that lead to successful games playing, learners are increasingly equipped to draw on this knowledge and experience in order to explore intuition and feelings, to see 'new possibilities', and thereby to participate in creative activity.

The concept of 'play' is closely associated with games. Playing is the generally accepted term for participation in games, even in professional sports. We 'play' tennis, volleyball, football, cricket, hockey and golf. Careers are built and earnings acquired through playing sport. The concept of successful 'play' at professional level involves not only skilful performance, but also calls for applications of mature cognitive, social, personal and emotional development. Building the foundations of these into the Physical Education curriculum for children is a prerequisite for successful games playing and for the transferring of relevant knowledge and practice into life in general. Where better to start than in primary school, engaging even the youngest children, according to their level of maturity and experience?

Play is also the accepted term for the general activity of children in their early years. Play consumes the majority of the waking part of each day, and play activities are essential to skilful movement acquisition and healthy development of children. Maria Montessori (1996) is often quoted for her claim that play is the work of the child. Time devoted to play enables infants to explore freely, to be active and spontaneous, to move to learn, and to learn to move. She also wrote that 'childhood constitutes the most important element in an adult's life, for it is in his early years that a man is made' (Montessori 1996: 83). This seems like a direct challenge to build on the early years of play and playfulness and to capitalise on every opportunity to build physical literacy into primary school education. With these factors in mind, consideration is now given to proposing ways and means of ensuring that the curriculum for games activities follows the POWER principles: *purpose* in providing opportunities for context and meaning-making, while building on previous knowledge and skills to introduce new; profiling the range of *opportunities* for games development across the curriculum; maintaining children's *well-being* as a central focus; offering a rich learning *environment*; and *revelling* in the achievements of all learners.

KEY ASPECTS

It would be helpful to remind yourself of the movement categories outlined in Chapter 2. Consider which of the movement categories shown there most lend themselves to learning through games-related activities. You could observe the children in your class and add other components of movement vocabulary for them to discover. Jess (cited in Griggs 2012: 40, 41) challenges us to create primary Physical Education programmes that are developmentally appropriate, inclusive, and connected and linked to children's lives.

Games activities for children in their Early Years, Key Stage 1 and Key Stages 2 are ideally suited to successfully meeting this challenge, where learning is built on children's prior experiences of unstructured, self-initiated, guided and structured play, and where new learning is set in the context of an enquiry-led, participatory and creative approach. Successful learning outcomes can be seen in children's achievements, their determination and sustained effort, delight and pleasure, evidence of growing confidence, and their self-guided motivation. Robinson (2001: 137) suggests that creative achievement can often emerge from within formal constraints. It is essential, therefore, that games activities are devised with a clear framework within which to build a wide range of skills and appropriate experiences, in a range of environments, with stimulating resources and in cooperation with significant others. These will scaffold children's learning and provide the backdrop for them to engage in the creative process of generating their own ideas, exploring positive avenues and dead ends, making judgements and producing outcomes that are of value.

■ **Figure 7.1** I am catching

Jess (cited in Griggs 2012: 42) reminds us that our pedagogy must engage all children in the learning process and must create authentic experiences.

We therefore explore the three elements of *locomotion*, *stability* and *object control* in continuing to provide the broad parameters for engaging all learners. *Locomotion*, which involves moving from one point to another, has a myriad of applications in games, whether to run fast between bases to score points, to move forwards and backwards to defend a playing area, or to accelerate and then stop to receive an approaching ball. *Stability* focuses on achieving and maintaining balance and control in static positions and in dynamic movement situations, as in holding an almost static balanced position from which to throw a beanbag into a hoop or to jump with control, while aiming a ball towards a high target. Learners need opportunities both to explore a wide range of activities involving locomotion and stability, and to experiment with and examine those that are particularly applicable in games situations, such as dodging, dribbling, jumping, chasing, retrieving, striking, fielding, weaving, chasing, marking, serving, scoring, pivoting, and changing speeds, levels and directions.

Object control develops the handling and management, travelling with, and sending and receiving of objects. It is in games activities that the development of, and proficiency in, object control is most readily promoted, such as can be seen in Figure 7.1.

All physically active games call on the skills of handling and controlling the wide range of objects that make up the school's resource provision, enabling learners to work on the spot and when travelling, when sending or receiving, and when playing alone or with others. Through games, children can extend and refine their manipulative skills, and then apply these in increasingly demanding situations, such as in creating games and in participating with other learners in cooperative and competitive situations. They can also transfer these experiences to extracurricular and community sport.

Proficiency in the manipulation of objects is a vital life skill both for basic independent survival and for engaging confidently in almost all other areas of the school curriculum, beyond Physical Education. Gaining access to, and managing, the myriad activities of daily life rely on efficient object control. Acquisition of efficient manipulative skill is dependent upon the development of the movement-related body systems, as previously discussed in Chapter 2. There, we found that physical development proceeds proximo-distally, from the centre of the body outwards from the shoulders to the elbows, and then to the wrists, hands and finally to the fingers. In the Early Years and Key Stage 1, children need to engage in frequent gross motor activity, such as is provided through object control in games activities, to promote and facilitate the development of fine motor control. In Chapter 2, we also found that children with sensorimotor and neuromotor delay may experience poor coordination between the limbs, with resultant lack of skill in the handling of objects. Delay in proprioceptive development and maturation of the eyes may also result in delay in managing hand-eye, foot-eye and foot-hand-eye coordination. What may seem like simple skills, normally easy for 5 year olds, such as running, standing on one foot without wobbling, hopping, skipping, throwing and catching a large ball, may be impossible for some children. Games activities can play a large part in nurturing their gradual development in these areas as children learn to blend object control with locomotion and stability. Games activities also facilitate aspects of cognitive, social and emotional development, calling on abilities such as to anticipate, respond and make quick decisions, change direction rapidly, cooperate with others, and compete fairly as they learn to lose and to win in ever-changing environments. Gardner (1993: xiv, 239–40) proposes seven forms of human intelligence, at least four of which can readily be enhanced through games activities, including bodily-kinaesthetic intelligence, spatial intelligence, and interpersonal and intrapersonal intelligences. Aspects of linguistic, mathematical and musical intelligences may also be embraced through games activities.

While *locomotion*, *stability* and *object control* constitute the ingredients for learning activities, it is the teaching approach that determines the potential for creativity in teaching and learning. At the extremes of their spectrum of teaching styles, Mosston and Ashworth (2002) propose a command style, at one end of the spectrum in which the teacher gives instructions and makes all the decisions, and the learner copies and complies (e.g. learners are all given the same size and shape of ball and copy the activity demonstrated by the teacher). This allows those who are capable of doing so to succeed, but does not provide them with work at a higher level of challenge. For those who are not capable of the activity, there is repeated reinforcement of failure. By way of contrast, in the guided discovery style, the teacher provides the learning objective and asks questions, and encourages learners to ask questions and to try out ideas that work towards achieving the learning objectives, thereby nurturing a 'can-do' culture of constant progression to new achievements. This approach enables learners of all abilities to experience active participation at their own level and of their own devising. This can produce unexpected results where creative learners work outside the conventional 'box' of traditional sport expectations, such as repeated 'skill drills', and they are free to develop movement competence, knowledge and active participation in games playing with understanding.

During Early Years and Key Stage 1, children can readily build on their physical competence and playful preschool years of uninhibited activity, when they were unencumbered by awareness of assessment of skill level, peer pressure and the self-criticism that may become challenges for older learners. This is the time to invest in a 'can-do' culture of developmental activities and to capitalise on perceived competence, vigorous participation, maximum activity, and freedom to learn and succeed in a stimulating and supportive environment. The Early Years and Key Stage 1 curriculum should offer maximum participation in frequent purposeful physical activity, both indoors and outdoors, whenever possible. Building a large movement vocabulary of skills, developing movement memory and the movement quality that results in skilful performance is best achieved through maximum hands-on experience in *object control*, *locomotion* and *stability*, and minimum time waiting for turns and sharing equipment.

Young learners enjoy discovering what they can do. Experimenting with the wide range of items to be found in the school games equipment collection is not only fun, but also offers a great range of experience in manipulation and management of each item. Adding the challenge of discovering the properties of each item, finding out what can be done with them and what sort of games they are best suited to, can reveal many surprises to both the creative teacher and the creative learner.

Scenario

A group of four trainee teachers was looking for a speedy and efficient way to lead their first session with a reception class, so that the children could start work immediately

■ **Figure 7.2** Equipment set out in one corner of the workspace

and independently, without the need for extensive explanation and instruction. In order to ensure that the learners could readily see and access all the resources available to them, they prepared as follows. In advance of the session, they made four sets of games equipment, with some items of each sort, such as balls, bats and markers, in each set. As far as possible, these were in coloured sets, namely red, yellow, green and blue, with small items stored in baskets and large items in nets.

Then, they placed the sets in the four corners of the workspace and laid out the equipment for easy access along the edges of the workspace (see Figure 7.2), so that children could readily access and select the equipment that they would need for each task (e.g. one child may select a beanbag, another a balloon ball and a third may choose a large ball). Bats, sticks and catchers were arranged such that the handles were ready to pick up. Finally, they set out enough coloured spots so that the children would be able to find one each as soon as they entered the hall.

As the learners came into the workspace, they were tasked to stand on a spot and run lightly on it and then around it. They then practised jumping on their spot, across it and around it. They were then asked to travel from one spot to another and to jump onto and off each spot before moving on and returning to their spot. Next,

▨ **Figure 7.3** Carrying out our equipment, ready to set it out for our group

they were tasked to choose one item from their own colour corner, return to their spot and try out what they could do with that object, keeping it close to them. The trainees observed that the spots ensured safe spacing, thus pre-empting and precluding the need to intervene and give reminders about spacing. They also noted that although the children could easily see the equipment, at first many did not know what to choose from the wide range of exciting alternatives! As the session progressed and they were given many more opportunities to put away one item and choose another, they found it easier to make quick selections, and, with encouragement from the trainee in 'their' corner, became increasingly adventurous in finding out the properties of each item. Travelling with the selected item around their own spot preceded locomotion around all the spots in the hall, still keeping the selected object close to them. Finally, learners showed their favourite activity, and then, as a group, packed away the equipment in their corner before returning to the classroom to change and talk about what they had learnt. In subsequent sessions, the children learnt to manage their own set of equipment and, increasingly, to work in safe spaces, well away from the stored equipment. They also learnt which resources were best suited to enable them to fulfil each task.

Exploring and building movement vocabulary and discovering the properties of resources in indoor and outdoor environments

In the 2014 National Curriculum for the UK at Key Stage 1 (DfE 2013: 221), accessing a broad range of opportunities is a prominent feature of the programme, including participation in team games and developing simple tactics for attacking and defending. Exploring and building movement vocabulary, establishing and mastering basic movements, and gaining knowledge and understanding offer rich aspirations for teachers and learners. This is the time to challenge learners to discover the properties of the resources that support games playing, and ways to exploit these, through breadth of creative exploration, trial and error. Then, through selection, repetition and practice, gradually to build up the skills, knowledge and understanding that lead to successful participation in games playing. Children thereby learn to select and apply skills appropriately, to participate in team games, and are introduced to simple tactics for attacking and defending.

Scenario

Have all the children in your class had opportunities to explore the following object control movement vocabulary? How can you help your learners to discover these and more, successfully, in a playful environment, both indoors and outdoors? Can they and you add to the following movement vocabulary?

Working *alone*, explore ways, with as wide a variety of objects as is available, to:

■   *Pass*: from hand to hand; around the waist, hips, chest, neck, head; around upper and lower right and left leg; over head – when standing and when sitting.

■ *Put down/release*: while sitting, lying, kneeling; while standing up; while walking; with two hands, right hand, left hand; onto a spot; into a free space; in front; to left and right sides; behind; by placing gently; by dropping.

■ *Pick up/grasp*: while sitting, lying, kneeling; while standing up; while walking; with two hands, right hand and left hand; in front; to left and right sides; behind; by placing gently; by dropping.

■ *Roll*: a ball to a rebound surface; with two hands, right hand, left hand; when sitting; when standing; forwards, backwards and under legs.

■ *Roll and collect*: from a rebound surface with two hands, right (R) hand, left (L) hand; make sequences of roll and collect using a combination of two hands, R hand and L hand.

■ *Roll along*: travel forwards; turn and collect – keeping a ball nearby and under control.

■ *Place up*: with two hands, R hand and L hand.

■ *Receive*: into two hands, R hand and L hand.

■ *Drop and catch*: into two hands, R hand and L hand.

■ *Bounce and catch*: with two hands, R hand and L hand.

■ *Push*: along using right and left foot; along using bat and stick on the forehand as well as the backhand side.

■ *Throw underarm*: R hand and L hand.

■ *Throw overarm*: R hand and L hand.

■ *Kick*: R foot and L foot.

■ *Strike*: using R and L hand/bat/stick.

■ *Aim*: to a target, by rolling, kicking, throwing, striking.

■ *Dribble*: continuous bounces; small, repeated, short kicks; taps using stick.

In addition to working forwards and in front, where it is easier to see and manage the object, can these activities also be achieved sideways to right and left, backwards, behind and around the body? Can learners manage to keep an object near to them when working indoors and then add distance when they work in the larger outdoor area? Can they also find ways to work with another learner as their partner?

Encouraging children to explore the properties of games equipment and find increasingly challenging ways to manipulate and control each item is a valuable ongoing learning objective, as is finding a balance between actually giving specific activities to try and enabling a discovery learning approach. The following is a bank of possible activities for children to experience, should they be needed, to guide their own discovery. The beanbag is the selected item here, as this is often found to be the easiest to manipulate and keep under control. Scarves and balloon balls are also relatively easy to manage, and if a child selects a quoit, Frisbee or even a spot (rubber throw-down marker), he or she can find many activities to try!

Here are 10 beanbag games to develop object control with locomotion and stability:

1   Pass a beanbag from hand to hand, with the added challenge of trying lots of ways to do this (e.g. in front, to the side, under the leg, round the body, over the head, while sitting, while lying, while travelling from spot to spot).

2   Carry a beanbag, travel to a spot, put it down, and at the next spot pick up another. In this game, look around for safe spaces, taking care not to bump into anyone else,

■ **Figure 7.4** The 'put down and pick up' game, with beanbags

especially when moving quickly to put down, pick up and travel, as in Figure 7.4. This game is also good for getting out of breath (extra spots can be laid out to ensure that learners always find a place to work).

3   Travel towards and give a beanbag to another learner while also receiving a beanbag from them. Vary the ways to give, receive and travel. The chart on ways to explore locomotion in Chapter 5 (p. 70) is also useful for increasing movement vocabulary in games activities.

4   Where can you balance a beanbag while on your spot and when travelling (e.g. head, back of hand, back when on hands and knees, stomach when on hands and feet, elbow, chest, on knee or foot when sitting or lying)?

5   Travel from one spot to another and show a different idea on each spot visited.

6   Send up and catch a beanbag when on a spot and when travelling.

7   Balance a beanbag on head/shoulder/bat/stick/spot while travelling.

8   Push a beanbag along the floor with a hand/foot/bat/stick.

9   Try out and show everything you can do with a beanbag and count how many activities were tried.

10   Choose two/three ways to use a beanbag and make a sequence.

While the examples above are confined to use of a beanbag for developing manipulative activities, the whole range of available equipment can be explored in similar ways, and there is no end to the possibilities of activity content and combinations of selected movement vocabulary to include in sequences.

Here is a suggested inventory of equipment for learners to explore:

▓   beanbags including animal shapes;
▓   balloon balls;
▓   scarves;

- quoits;
- small, medium and large foam balls for indoor use;
- size 3 footballs for outdoor use;
- medium size, low bounce inflatable plastic balls;
- small rugby balls;
- airflow balls;
- foam discs/Frisbees;
- low bounce, soft tennis balls;
- hoops;
- catchers;
- plastic bats (variety of sizes and shapes, including cricket);
- short unihoc sticks;
- small strung rackets (e.g. badminton and tennis shape);
- shuttles;
- skipping ropes;
- tees;
- rubber spots and strips;
- flexi-cones;
- hands and feet markers,
- skittles; and
- small goals with nets and low goals with rings.

Developing locomotion for games activities

In a previous National Curriculum, the three categories of activities for young children were 'travel-with', 'send' and 'receive'. Travel-with is a useful concept, especially in the context of working towards those invasion games in which two teams aim to score goals at opposite ends of a playing area, or where, for example, the management of a racket, bat or stick is integral to the locomotion, as in net and field games.

Exploring travel-with

Creative learners could be guided again to experiment with some of the ways to explore locomotion as outlined in Chapter 5 (p. 70) to discover which can be used for making up games of travel-with, by selecting and experimenting with as many items as possible in their equipment corner. The objective would be to keep the items near to them and under control as they travel. They might also find that they can use the ideas in Table 7.1 as a basis for their discoveries.

Activities such as these may not always appear to relate directly to games playing, but are invaluable in developing manipulative skills and in enhancing locomotion in conjunction with object control and stability. Valuable experience is gained through using imagination to determining the suitability of each item of games equipment for making up games and for learning to manage their selected activities in the context of the indoor or outdoor environment and work surface, and in relation to all other learners sharing the same space.

■ **Table 7.1** Some ideas for travel-with

carrying	rolling	bouncing	sending up and catching	pushing along/dribbling	jumping
in the hand	right hand	bounce and	right and left	by hand	with a rope
in the hands	left hand	catch	hand	with a foot	
on the head		continuous	both hands	with a bat	
on the back		bounce	send up,	with a stick	
between the		right hand	allow to	with a catcher	
knees		left hand	bounce		
		both hands	and catch		
			send up, clap		
			and catch		

Progressions in learning specific skills

Specific games skills, such as catching, throwing, kicking and striking, can be developed through game-like progressions, rather than being presented as whole skills, particularly for learners who are not ready to perform whole skills. For example, catching grows out of many of the activities considered above, including grasping, picking up, receiving a rolled object, placing up and allowing an object to land back into the two hands, dropping and grasping, bouncing and catching, sending a ball up and letting it bounce before catching it, and sending an object to a wall and catching it from a bounce. Learning to catch a ball sent by another person is best achieved if the ball is fed underarm, so that it bounces and comes more slowly up from the floor into the hands of the receiver. As hand-eye coordination may not be fully developed in the early years, some learners will achieve catching much later than others.

As with catching, striking skills can readily be established through floor-level activities, such as pushing along a large ball or hoop, or sending a ball along with small kicks. Adding a bat extends the arm and thereby adds challenge to hand-eye coordination. Carrying a beanbag, shuttle, quoit, scarf or Frisbee on a bat, with the palm facing downwards, as well as upwards, introduces the idea of backhand, as well as forehand, as does sending an object up from the bat and catching it again on the bat. Similarly, learners can explore forehand and backhand as they push a ball along the floor with a bat. Examples of games that increase experience, establish a movement pattern, and encourage repetition and practice include, for example:

'How many times can you bounce the ball without stopping?'
'Can you beat that score?'
'Can you travel as well?'
'How quickly can you roll the ball to the wall and receive it five times?'
'How can you make this game harder and still succeed?'
'How can you make this game easier when it is too difficult to score?'

<u>What I like doing</u>

I like   *to bounce.*

This is my picture of what I like doing

I like this because   *it is a   special   game*

My name is   *Taher*

■ **Figure 7.5** What I like doing, by Taher

<u>What I like doing</u>

I like *bounceing the ball*

This is my picture of what I like doing

I like this because *the teacher tauht nicly*

My name is *Ansh*

■ **Figure 7.6** What I like doing, by Ansh

Developing movement memory and movement quality

Creating sequences of manipulative activities helps learners to develop their movement memory as they try to join one activity to another. The freedom of unstructured practice, so important in developing movement vocabulary, becomes more constrained as learners meet new challenges around choice and decision-making. Building a sequence extends thinking beyond random practice into decision-making about the choice of activities to put into a sequence, the order of the activities, how to perform the first idea, how to link with the second, and then how to perform the second. Learners will also need to decide when to end the first activity and, at the same time, must anticipate and then lead into and execute the second.

Repetition and practice then facilitate the development of movement quality, as learners become familiar with the chosen activities and practise recalling both of the individual ingredients in the same order, along with the link that combines them. Controlled and still starts and ends to sequences and smooth, flowing transitions further enhance quality performance. Enabling learners to increase the complexity of their sequences, either in length or content, adds further challenge. Teachers may wish to refer to the *movement dimensions* chart in Chapter 6 (p. 89, Figure 6.3) as a possible resource for selecting ideas to encourage learners to apply in helping them to develop movement quality in games activities. For example, learners may be ready to try adding a change of direction into their work, to go sideways or backwards, as well as forwards. If their sequences are always slow, they could be encouraged to include an activity that is done quickly while maintaining control. If they always work in normal upright postural positions, they might be encouraged to include an activity at a higher or lower level. This also allows for transfer of relevant knowledge and experience from one aspect of Physical Education learning to another.

Cooperation and competition

For younger children, working alone provides for maximum hands-on experience and time spent on the selected task. Once learners are asked to share equipment, for example, using a small ball to throw and catch to one another, unless both players are competent in both activities, the learning task may be too difficult to achieve, the game breaks down, the hands-on time may not have been maximised, and there seems to be no recognisable achievement. Useful progress is made when, to be more successful, they decide to find something that they can both catch, such as a balloon ball, or they change the activity to rolling, or decide that standing nearer to each other is more successful.

However, as games playing often calls for the ability to cooperate with others to achieve a common aim, early introduction of cooperative activity encourages peer empathy in social situations, sharing ideas and the fun of achieving something together. Strategies for working in pairs can readily be established with young learners, particularly when each player continues to control his or her own object. For example, one learner can show another player an idea that they can then both try to do at the same time, and then they can swap over the lead and find that they can make a sequence of two activities. They can also learn to consider where best to position themselves to work together. This could include facing each other, or starting side by side, or by taking turns at leading and following, or by travelling towards and away from each other. For example, while working side by side, each player could roll their ball forwards as they travel forwards, pick up their ball and then send the ball up, clap and catch it three times while standing still. Attempting to perform this sequence in unison calls not only for skill in each selected activity, but also awareness, observation and cooperation in decision-making with regard to content, linking and timing. Questioning and support from the teacher can enable even young children gradually to manage challenging concepts such as these.

Competition for young children

Personal challenge constitutes a sound starting place to learn about some aspects of competition, including improving on past achievement, managing failure as well as success and recognising the importance of fair play. Games such as 'beating my previous score' challenge past achievement and also put pressure on the performance of the activity, such that the outcome may not always be as successful as previously. 'I mustn't try too hard to toss my beanbag into the net, because it always goes the wrong way when I do!' Games played one against one enable both players to continue developing their own personal challenge while also experiencing different roles. In the game seen in Figure 7.7, one player tries to throw three beanbags into one or other of the hoops, while the opponent tries to intercept and catch the beanbags as they pass. The players then change places, so that they both practise the role of attacker and defender.

Recognising fair play is evident, for example, when a learner always starts at the same distance from the target when rolling a ball between two skittles and only counts a goal when the ball actually goes between the skittles. Competition that is set in the context of a positive learning climate, whether competing with oneself, with others or against others, promotes outcomes that should always be worthwhile learning experiences, whether through winning or losing. When the definition of a 'team' is seen as a minimum of two players, there is a wealth of experience to be gained in Key Stage 1. Although young children need plenty of time in hands-on experience with games equipment, when, for example, a ball

■ **Figure 7.7** We are attacking and defending

is shared between two players, new learning develops around the role of the player not in possession of the ball. Thus, the decrease in hands-on experience at that time in a session is superseded by new learning opportunities, such as being in a good place to receive, watching the ball and getting ready to receive. Teams of two can create games that they can play successfully as team members together. They can then teach another team to play their game and finally play one team against the other. For example:

> My partner and I bounced a ball to each other until we had caught it 10 times altogether. When we played against another team, they won because they were quicker. They chose rolling to each other and we won because we finished first! Our teacher asked us how to be quicker in our game, because we didn't catch the ball every time. We tried again. If the bouncer sends a good bounce, it is easy to catch.

This is a really useful learning experience, because it is often the failed catch that is blamed for defeat, whereas the failed catch is often due to the inaccuracy, over-enthusiasm or lack of empathy of the sender.

Target games

Playing games that score points or goals not only helps to reinforce object control and accuracy, but also provides for challenge and a sense of achievement, through learning to make games harder and easier and through finding fair ways to score more points:

> In the hoop and basket game, we started near to our target, and each time we scored a point we moved back one step. When we missed, we moved one step forward. In the skittles game, we started with wide goals and when we scored a goal, we moved the goals nearer to each other. When we missed, we moved the goals further apart.

▓ **Figure 7.8** We made these target games

Here are more target games to play, with examples shown in Figure 7.8:

■ beanbag into hoop by hand;
■ shuttle into basket from a bat;
■ ball into bucket from a catcher;
■ ball between skittles by rolling;
■ ball between skittles by kicking;
■ ball between skittles by striking.

Can you make up others to play outdoors with small goals and low rings with nets?

Learning to move towards a target while also receiving and sending is a useful games strategy to develop as early as possible. This involves being able to get into a balanced position to receive with sufficient control to look ahead, and be ready to send to the next player and then immediately to travel on. Below in Figures 7.9 and 7.10 are two ideas for games that give learners this experience. Once they have mastered the pattern of the games, they can decide on which equipment to use and which type of send and receive they will try. Here are some suggestions for sending:

■ roll a ball;
■ kick a ball;
■ bounce a ball;
■ throw a ball;
■ push with a unihoc stick;
■ send a beanbag from a bat;
■ push along the ground with a bat.

■ **Figure 7.9** Look ahead, pass ahead and move ahead

Figure 7.9 shows a 'look ahead, pass ahead, move ahead' game with four players:

Player 1 sends the ball across to Player 2 and then runs across to the back of the opposite line, behind Player 4.

Player 2 receives the ball, sends it across to Player 3 and runs across to stand behind Player 3.

Player 3 receives the ball, sends it across to Player 4 and runs across to stand behind Player 1.

Player 4 receives the ball, sends it across to Player 2 and runs across to stand behind Player 2.

Below (Figure 7.10) is a 'look ahead, pass ahead, move ahead' game with two players. The pattern of this game is that the players start side by side and about a metre apart:

Player 1 starts with the ball.

Player 2 travels forwards and Player 1 sends the ball diagonally forwards to Player 2.

Player 1 travels forwards as Player 2 receives the ball, looks for Player 1 and sends the ball diagonally across to Player 1.

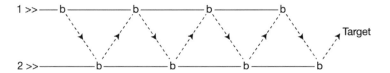

■ **Figure 7.10** A 'look ahead, pass ahead, move ahead' game

This game both builds from the pattern of the previous game and challenges players to control their forward run in order to receive the ball with control and then pass it diagonally. Players might solve the apparent complexity of games such as this by deciding that to be successful, they will start with travel by walking and send by rolling. Gradually, they can decide from their bank of experience to introduce more speed, different equipment, and ways of sending and receiving.

Proposals for the 2014 National Curriculum (www.education.gov.uk/schools) intend that learners should become increasingly competent and confident, and be able to engage in competitive (both against self and against others) and cooperative physical activities in a range of increasingly challenging situations. They should also:

■ participate in team games, developing simple tactics for attacking and defending;
■ develop competence to excel in a broad range of physical activities;
■ be physically active for sustained periods of time;
■ engage in competitive sports and activities; and
■ lead healthy, active lives.

SUMMARY

In this chapter, we have taken account of these proposals. We have maintained awareness of enabling learners to make progress on their physical literacy journey in physical competence, knowledge and understanding, while also enhancing the motivation and confidence of all learners. We have considered ways in which the creative teacher can enable learners to explore a wide range of games equipment; build movement vocabulary; progressively develop movement memory and movement quality through object control, locomotion and stability; create and play games alone, in pairs and in groups; experience losing and winning; develop game-playing strategies; and find fair ways to be successful.

FURTHER READING

Griggs, G. (2007) *Physical Education: The Essential Toolkit for Primary School Teachers*, Blackburn: ePRINT.

Visual Learning Company (2007) *Games Activities*, DVD, www.visuallearning.co.uk.

Youth Sport Trust (2012) *Start to Move*, available at: www.starttomovezone.com (accessed 1 January 2014).

CHAPTER 8

DEVELOPING GAMES

INTRODUCTION

Learners bring to Key Stage 2 vast movement ability and knowledge, developed from their infancy, Early Years and Key Stage 1 experiences. For most children, much of their junior school education can be considered as the 'skill hungry' years, coming between the rapid growth periods that preceded their arrival in junior school and prior to the approaching adolescent growth spurt. Basic movement patterns will have been established, along with coordination and control, and learners can readily call on their extensive movement vocabulary, wide range of physical skills, increasingly mature movement memory, and knowledge of movement quality. Through games activities, they will have found out about *object control* and will have gained skills in manipulation of a wide range of games equipment, as well as those aspects of *locomotion* and *stability* that facilitate games playing. From their earliest days in school, learners will have created sequences with game-like content, will have found ways to progress the achievement of specific games skills such as footwork, catching, throwing, striking and kicking, and will have played games created by themselves and others. They will have found ways to manage and share the working space safely, to take responsibility for themselves, and to work alongside and with other learners, in pairs and small groups. They will have learnt about questioning, and about evaluating and recording their experiences and progress, and about how to cooperate and compete and build their motivation and confidence as they travel along their physical literacy journey. This chapter is therefore intended to build upon these achievements, and to promote creative teaching and learning for children aged 7–11 years through games playing.

A much-used model of games teaching, known as the technical model, involved teaching the skills required for a named game (e.g. dribbling and driving for hockey, and forehand, backhand, serve, volley and smash for tennis) in isolation before playing the game. This method suited those learners capable of mastering technical skills at that moment in time, but did not always enable less physically competent learners to succeed. While there is an important place for practice and performance of technically accurate models of named skills, these alone do not make games players. Griffin and Butler (2005: 40) state: 'The expected outcome of the technical model is that students will become skilful performers.' They go on to explain that if the teaching focus has been on kicking skills for football, learners expect to kick when a game is introduced, and the result is often that everyone crowds around the ball in order to continue what has been taught. This model of teaching also relies more on teacher direction and less on learner participation, other than their attempts to perform the physical skills, as directed. They go on to suggest (Griffin and Butler 2005: 57) that learners 'would become more proficient games players if they learned to understand the decisions to be made during game play'.

The 2014 National Curriculum helpfully heralds a more rounded approach to teaching and learning through Physical Education, as indicated in the opening statements for Key Stage 2, which include: 'They should enjoy communicating, collaborating and competing with each other. They should develop an understanding of how to improve . . . and learn how to evaluate and recognise their own success' (DfE 2013: 199). With reference to games, it is further stated that pupils should be taught to 'play competitive games, modified where appropriate . . . and apply basic principles suitable for attacking and defending'. Bailey and Macfadyen (2000: 46) remind us that competition forms a distinctive feature of Physical Education. While many children enjoy competition, others do not. They go on to state: 'competition might form the environment of participation but should not be the goal; it is the medium, not the message'. This, and the more open National Curriculum model above, chime well with the QCA (2007) framework of personal and thinking skills (see also Ankers and Dixon 2009).

The QCA framework is made up of six skill sets, all of which are relevant in some measure in learning through games in Key Stage 2, and all of which constitute worthwhile aspirations for the creative teacher and learner. The aim is for learners increasingly to become:

■ independent enquirers;
■ creative thinkers;
■ reflective learners;
■ team workers;
■ self-managers; and
■ effective participators.

Building games experience at Key Stage 2 that is based on nurturing learners in these skills will enable them to make significant progress in their lifelong physical literacy journey. Throughout this chapter, the underlying intention is that learners are guided to develop learning and thinking skills, and to build their motivation and commitment to active participation in games, so that they enter Key Stage 3 with confidence. The approach taken is that learners continue to mature in physical competence and that they understand the factors that constitute the playing of games. The approach also embraces opportunities for learners to develop cognitively in knowledge and understanding, socially in their intrapersonal and interpersonal intelligences (Gardner 1993), and in their emotional intelligence towards becoming 'self-directed, self-starters, highly motivated and excellent communicators' (Coleman, cited in Robinson 2001: 139).

Baroness Campbell, Head of UK Sport, was reported to have told delegates at an education conference that thousands of pupils are entering Key Stage 3 unable to jump, throw a ball or run (Campbell 2013). Ideally, this would be addressed in preschool, Early Years and Key Stage 1, as well as in Key Stage 2. Special programmes are being run in many schools for children with delayed movement development to enable them to improve their manipulative skills and coordination. As a result, many children also gain in confidence and motivation, and feel better able to participate in games, as well as school activities in general. Drew and Atter (2008), on the title page of their book *Can't Play, Won't Play*, offer 'simply sizzling ideas to get the ball rolling for children with dyspraxia'.

In his poem 'Take Me Out of the Ball Game', Nathan (2007) presents the plight of one such child in a baseball game:

> Take me out of the ball game.
> It's my turn up to bat.
> I can't hit the ball, which is no surprise.
> I'm too frightened to open my eyes
> And I heard strike three whizzing past me.
> If we don't win, I'm to blame
> For it's one, two, three strikes, I'm out
> When I play this game.

The challenge for the creative teacher is to develop a rounded curriculum, fit for purpose, that engages all learners, including those who may have poor perceptions of their physical competence.

KEY ASPECTS

■ **Figure 8.1** We are playing korfball

Scenario

In the classroom before a games-playing session, a trainee teacher asked her group of Year 4 children, 'What makes a game?'

Responses included: 'having fun', 'winning', 'knowing the rules', 'playing alone', 'getting a big score', 'being outdoors', 'getting the ball', 'scoring' and 'being in a team'.

She went on to ask them what rules they would decide on before starting to play a ball game. The children discussed this, and agreed that you need to know:

1   where to play and where the boundaries are;
2   what equipment to use;
3   how to start;
4   how to score;
5   what happens if the ball goes outside the area; and
6   whether you need any other special rules.

The playground session started with a warm-up game of 'turn-over'. The learners set out flexi-cones all over the playing area and then travelled, first by jogging and then by running, from cone to cone to turn them over. In a timed game, they counted how many cones they could turn in two minutes. This game involved spatial awareness to dodge past other players, cardio-respiratory activity, and keeping their score.

■ **Figure 8.2** A 'turn-over' game

The session then progressed to playing a striking and fielding game in fours, with two fielders on one team and the bowler and striker on the other team. They set down spots to mark the bowler and batter's positions, and a cone as the base to run to and from. The bowler and batter had three goes each and then the teams changed over. They scored one run each time they reached the cone and came back to base before the fielders gave the ball back to the bowler. They decided that nobody was 'out', but that what counted was getting runs. One group decided to play with a soft outdoor ball and a wooden bat. The other group of four played a similar game but they chose a large ball and to play by kicking. Part way through the session, they showed each other their choice of game and then changed over to play the other game.

■ **Figure 8.3** This is our striking and fielding game

Although it might have been easier to strike the ball from a tee, they decided that it was more important to practise batting the ball sent by a bowler and for the bowler to practise accurate bowling that their teammate could hit.

Afterwards, they reported that they needed rules for 2, 3 and 4 above. They also needed rule 6 to know how many turns to have each, that nobody was out and also that you ran each time even if you did not hit the ball. They also thought that it would be good to practise more bowling so that the team of striker and kicker would have better chances to score, and they wanted to practise more striking and kicking so that they could make the ball go further away and give the fielders more work to do. When asked what they liked about the games, they had all enjoyed playing and felt that they had tried hard and got out of breath lots of times. They liked having their partner on the same team so that they could help each other to score more points. They thought that the kicking game was harder to play. These learners seemed to demonstrate many of the qualities outlined in the QCA Learning and Thinking Skills outlined above. They seemed to show qualities of independent enquirers, reflective learners, team workers, self-managers and effective participators. They were also aware of the need for improving their skill in the techniques of the game and of the necessity for rules that help them to know and understand how to play the game. As a group, they also showed awareness of varying roles that participants take when playing this game, and they felt that there was plenty more to learn about games in Key Stage 2.

Game types and game strategies

Scenario

As part of a Year 5 cross-curricular project on 'Games, Sports and Pastimes', which followed from the 2012 Olympic Games, one aspect was to research playground games of the past, such as ring toss, conkers, marbles, grandmothers' footsteps, and examples of games with rhymes. The children found Iona and Peter Opie's (1969) book, *Children's Games in Street and Playground*, to be very helpful, and they compared the games they discovered there and from many other sources with playground games in 2013. They also discussed why some games stay the same, such as skipping, and why other games disappear or change. A second aspect of the project was to look at the contents of the baskets and sacks of games equipment for Key Stage 1, and study sports equipment catalogues in order to draw up a list of additional items that are needed in Key Stage 2. Having costed their selection against a budget, they decided to recommend the following items:

- size 3 and 4 balls for outdoor high-fives netball, five-a-side football, and mini and touch rugby;
- small five-a-side-type goals with nets;
- junior height netball posts with rings and nets;
- ball pumps and adaptors;
- canes;
- floor agility ladders;
- hockey sticks, soft balls and pads;
- bibs and bands;
- Frisbees;
- coated foam balls in various sizes for indoor use;
- size 3 footballs for outdoor use;
- size 3 netballs for outdoor use;
- size 3 rugby balls;
- some size 4 balls;
- soft hockey balls;
- low-bounce tennis balls;
- rackets – short-handled badminton and tennis;
- rounders bats – padded;
- cricket bats and free-standing stumps;
- floor agility ladders;
- short tennis nets and posts; and
- tees.

A third aspect of the project was to list all the games that adults play, and to consider which would be useful to learn about games playing through Physical Education in primary school. The children amassed a long list of games and concluded that some are like one other, such as basketball, korfball and netball; rounders, softball and baseball; and hockey, floorball, goalball and ice hockey. Pupil inquisitiveness, questioning and discussion led to the idea of categorising games, and the following groupings emerged as a way forward for trying to sort into categories games that could be played in school:

- target games;
- games that need a net or wall;
- striking and fielding games; and
- invasion games.

We have already considered target games in the previous chapter, where learners in Key Stage 1 discovered the importance of accuracy when aiming towards targets and gained wide-ranging experience in manipulative skills through object control. They were guided by their teacher to create their own games by choosing a target, an object to send to the target and a way to send that object, and they also decided how near to or how far from the target to start to be successful, yet also to be challenged. One game was to throw a large ball into a low goal with a net. The second was to kick a ball between markers. The third game involved a racket and ball, to send a ball between markers. The final choice of game was to aim beanbags into a hoop on the ground. Learners were able to challenge themselves to make the game harder, by moving further from their target. Other strategies that continue in Key Stage 2 include making games harder by changing the size, texture and shape of the object to be sent (e.g. a puck, shuttle or rugby ball), or changing the way it would be sent (e.g. using the non-dominant hand or foot to send, aiming the shuttle from a racket, or sending the rugby ball backwards). Racket games could include both forehand and backhand, with a bounce before the ball is struck, and to increase the challenge, volleys, in which the ball is struck before it bounces. For some games, the size of the target could be reduced, by narrowing the distance between the markers, to add challenge to accuracy. Learners might add locomotion to their game, by travelling before aiming. This increases cardio-vascular activity and the speed of the game and can also lead to inaccuracies and further exercise while retrieving the stray balls that by-passed the target! Similar games can be played indoors when markers are placed against walls, which then serve as barriers to help keep the ball under control.

Experience in target games helps in developing accuracy in many other games situations. For example, placing the ball or shuttle out of the reach of the opponent and within the playing area, such as in tennis, badminton, volleyball, table tennis and squash, helps to ensure winning that point. Also, mastering the ability to send a ball or puck accurately to a member of the same team, such as in water polo, ice hockey, netball and lacrosse, both progresses the object in its journey towards the target and may provide an opportunity for a goal to be scored immediately. A further challenge to accuracy is that the team member may not be standing still waiting to receive, and therefore, to be successful, the pass must travel in the direction of the estimated point of receipt and must be sent with just enough power to be receivable.

The games that the learners listed in the target game category, in addition to the games that they and others created, included darts, pool, billiards, archery, putting and golf.

They suggested that net/wall games are those that are played over a net or against a wall, so they suggested tennis and badminton. Squash and volleyball were also added. There was a discussion around the difference between striking games and invasion games, since some games seemed to fit into two categories, such as hockey, which is played by striking the ball, as is rounders. The discussion was also not fully informed by the definition that invasion games involve crossing the territory of an opposing team, since, for example, the runner who is in the batting team in rounders goes all around the playing area occupied by the fielding team. Once they were asked what is special about hockey that is also special about football and netball, but different from rounders, the learners worked out that it must be something to do with how and where points are scored. It was finally decided that in invasion games, there is usually a goal at each end and players score into the goal of the opposing team and try to prevent the opposing team from scoring in their goal, such as high-fives netball, five-a-side football, and touch and mini rugby. Striking games that they

■ **Figure 8.4** What are we learning about?

discussed as possibilities for use in school included stoolball, kwik cricket and French cricket, as well as rounders and adapted baseball.

In Key Stage 2, much can be learnt about skills and strategies for playing net/wall games. Carrying and manipulating a beanbag or ball on a bat or racket, like in a frying pan, with the palm upwards and the palm downwards, begins to introduce the idea of forehands and backhands. Forehand and backhand can also be practised while dribbling a ball along the ground with light taps, with a bat or racket. Striking a ball against a wall with forehand and backhand reinforces the need to turn sideways to hit and to transfer the weight from the back foot to the front foot. In Figure 8.4, two learners are practising forehand and backhand. The other two are thinking about playing 'catch tennis' over the strip by sending and receiving. They chose a large ball to make it easy, and they tried to make the ball bounce on their partner's side of the strip, so that it came up from the ground into their partner's hands, to make it even easier to catch, as they wanted to make a big score of catches. When asked how to make the game more difficult, they would try moving to a new space after sending, so that the sender had to look before sending, which also made the game more active. All games-playing benefits from skilful *locomotion* and *stability*, underpinned by good footwork, which enables learners to accelerate, decelerate, stop, and change directions and levels rapidly and safely, in response to the constantly changing environment, often among other players who are also on the move. Gaining experience in controlling balance both when still and when moving helps learners to achieve the effective marking, serving, aiming, dodging, feinting, weaving, jumping and landing, which are essential ingredients in games playing. Fun can be had with floor ladders, through encouraging learners to create speedy step patterns from one end to the other, and travelling forwards, sideways to the right and left and backwards, to increase their agility.

Invasion games are conceptually more difficult to master, due to the complexity of the tasks required to take an object through the area of play, which is also occupied by their opponents, in order to score in their opponents' goal. Players need to understand how

▪ **Figure 8.5** We chose unihoc sticks and a squashy ball

to play both as attackers and also defenders, often with little time spent in each role. In attack, learners need to know how to get into a good position to receive the ball, when to move into a free space to draw a defender away from the ball, to free the space for others to receive the ball, and when to mark opponents so that other team members can take the ball towards the goal. They also need to know how to proceed when their opponents gain possession of the ball, and what to do to regain control. In addition, they need techniques for travelling-with, controlling, receiving and passing the ball accurately.

The game in Figure 8.5 is linear in shape. The learners next tried working in pairs, and were guided to find out how to include travelling when not in possession of the ball. The game that emerged was that Player 1 would pass the ball to Player 2 and would then run a little way into a new space, stop there, get ready to receive the ball, and look at Player 2. In the meantime, Player 2 would have received and controlled the ball and then looked up to locate Player 1, standing ready to receive, before passing. As they became more proficient, they speeded up the game. They then played in a grid with two other pairs, each playing the same game, but now everyone had to avoid interfering with the two other games. This activity enabled one learner to experience ways of supporting another and cooperating to achieve as many successful moves and passes as possible.

Once a third player in the role of defender is introduced into the game, the challenge of keeping possession of the ball is greatly increased. Learners have to work out how to avoid the defence, by ensuring that the defence is not in the space between them.

Some useful progressions for learners to consider, in finding out and gaining successful experience in this, is by placing restrictions on the involvement of the defender:

A1

      D   Target

A2

In this pattern of play, A1 and A2 are trying to travel-with and pass the ball to each other, to reach the target. At first, the defender, D, occupies the centre of the area, but does not move or attempt to intercept. The learners change roles frequently, as they find ways to get past the defender as attackers, on their way to the target and to think about what they will do to get the ball when playing as the defender. Once they are successful in this game, the defender could try to intercept from the limited position of being able to move just from side to side, to block the space but not attempt to touch the ball. Thereafter, the defender could be free to move forward and back, as well as side to side, still without attempting to touch the ball. Finally, the defender could try to touch the ball. They might then play a scoring game of one point to each of the attackers if they reach the target, or one point to the defender who manages to touch the ball. Once the ball is touched by the defender, the game ends. As the players change roles, they can keep a tally of their own points achieved in both roles. Learners are then ready to find fair and safe ways to intercept and gain possession, bringing into the game their dodging skills, quick footwork, ability to change direction to block free spaces, and, where relevant, jumping to intercept the path of the ball, as in netball.

In Figure 8.6, the players are discussing how to gain possession of the ball fairly, without tackling the stick of the opponent.

■ **Figure 8.6** Thinking about intercepting

Use of grids

Learners can create playing areas suited to the game in hand by placing spots or strips to indicate boundaries. School playgrounds and fields can also be marked into grids, and existing markings, such as on a netball court, can be adapted for class use. Figure 8.8 is an example of use of grids for developing invasion games, where the learning objectives are to practise attack, defence and scoring. Learning to play 'off the ball' creates more open space and makes the task of defending harder, especially with only two defenders against three attacking players. The equipment selected for these games was for unihoc, netball and bounceball.

Figures 8.7 and 8.10 illustrate games for three attacking players versus two defending players, in which the learners are finding out how to make space to receive the ball and keep the ball away from the defenders. Having practised the role of attack, they were later guided to consider how to defend, intercept and prevent the attackers from scoring.

Through the games in Figure 8.8, the learners were focusing on:

■ goal scoring in games 1, 3 and 5, when working alone or cooperatively in pairs or threes; and

■ strategies for attack and defence in games 2, 4 and 6 in order to create opportunities to score goals.

■ **Figure 8.7** Finding out about attack and defence

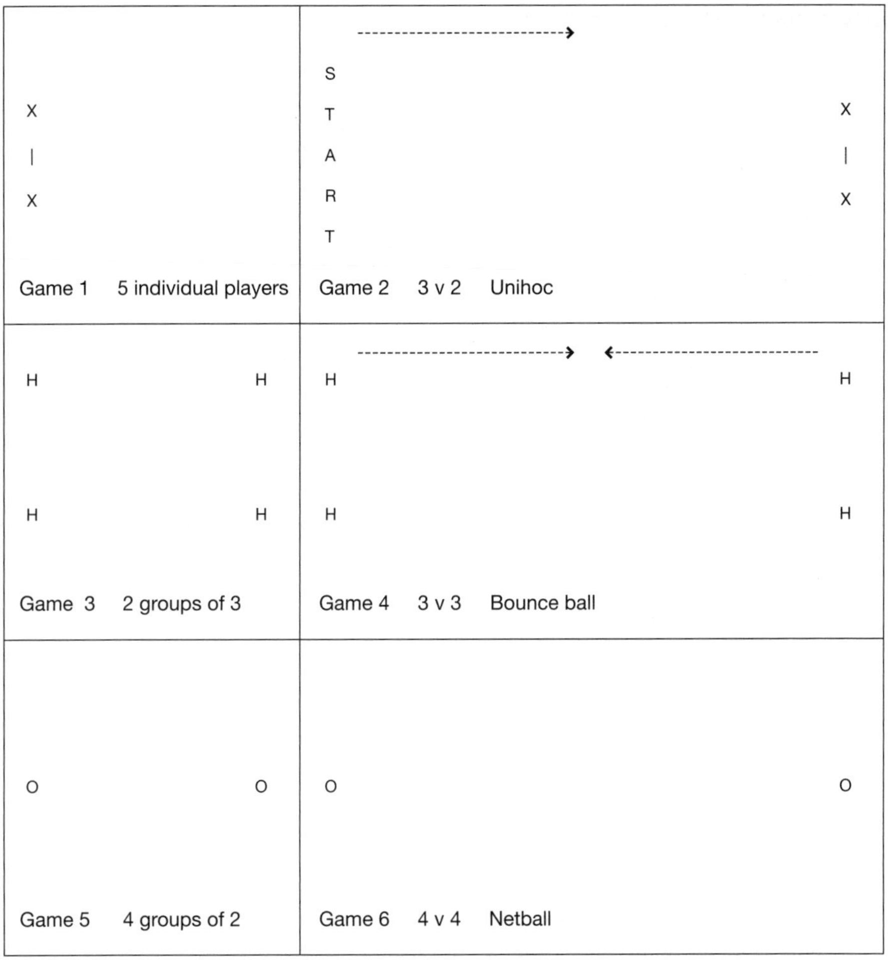

	---------------------------->
X X	S
| |	T
X X	A
	R
	T
Game 1 5 individual players	**Game 2** 3 v 2 Unihoc
H H	----------------------------> <----------------------------
	H H
H H	H H
Game 3 2 groups of 3	**Game 4** 3 v 3 Bounce ball
O O	O O
Game 5 4 groups of 2	**Game 6** 4 v 4 Netball

Game 1
5 individual players with unihoc sticks and soft outdoor balls each practise goal scoring from all points in their area, from standing shots and shots taken on the move, using push pass and drive

Game 2
3 attacking players make spaces to pass the ball, defeating the 2 opponents, to score a goal. When the stick of a defence player touches the ball the game restarts. Players change positions frequently

Game 3
Each group of 3 players has a ball and works as a team, passing the ball, using all the space and placing the ball into the hoop at each end

Game 4
Each team of 3 players aims to score points by placing the ball into one of the 2 hoops in their opponents end. Dribbling the ball is permitted and passing to a team member is by bounce passes

Game 5
Players practise short passes, without travelling with the ball, to their partner and scoring in the low goal rings with nets

Game 6
Two teams of 4 players aim to score into the low goal rings in their opponents end, using passing and without travelling with the ball

Figure 8.8 Use of grids for creating and developing invasive games

Learners could use this set of six games for several sessions, and during each session might play just games 1 and 3, or games 2 and 4, or games 4 and 6, changing from one to the other several times. Alternatively, they might play more than one pair of games.

■ **Figure 8.9** In *Game Sense* skills are learnt within the game (Light 2013)

These learners enjoy playing football, are familiar with the rules of various modified football games, and are gaining competence in appropriate techniques and game-playing tactics. This enabled them to concentrate on such aspects as the fundamental concept of decision-making in games playing, particularly with the dynamic nature of the game with its constantly changing environment of moving players and unpredictability of the pathway of the ball. In game-centred learning, the players can concentrate on which decisions need to be made, such as 'When will I . . .?', 'Where will I . . .?', 'What are the risks?', and 'Which option shall I go for?' In situations such as this, the creative teacher becomes the creator of problem situations and the facilitator for finding solutions, rather than a model to be copied. By pausing the game and recreating the point at which the game broke down, learners can explore other options and, with hindsight, make alternative and better decisions that can be tried once the game restarts.

In relation to assessment, Jones and Wyse (2004) suggest that creativity is difficult to measure and quantify, but offers the following suggestions for focusing consideration and observation, such as:

■ using questioning that is open-ended, challenging and capable of generating ideas;
■ noting thinking that is imaginative, that searches for alternatives, is lateral rather than linear, and ideas that are innovative;
■ observing pupil responses that demonstrate independent thinking and a willingness to take risks;

■ **Figure 8.10** Hockey, three players against two

- noting learners who are absorbed and excited in their learning;
- valuing responses; and
- offering opportunities for collaboration, reflection and review.

These criteria are entirely appropriate in creative teaching and learning through games playing. Assessment for learning, such as this 'builds learning power' (Frapwell and Caldecott 2011: 45), through active involvement of the learners and through enabling them to discover more about learning to learn.

Let us return again to remind ourselves of the POWER principles. Here, children are supported and challenged to explore *purpose* and skills in games playing, but also meaning-making and connection. *Opportunities* are provided within games for children to connect to other Physical Education work, and potentially also, to other curriculum areas. Children's *well-being*, especially regarding building resilience, is key, and this relates to the development of an appropriate, positive *environment*, where all are keen to *revel* in each other's achievements.

SUMMARY

In his book, *Game Sense*, Light (2013: 23) writes about the benefits that can be gained through games playing, including enhancing social interaction and promoting achievement through active participation and a collective approach to problem-solving. He suggests that learners enjoy knowing what a game is about, knowing that they are able to contribute and knowing that they are empowered in interacting and decision-making.

In this chapter we have built from the Introduction to Games in Key Stage 1, along with the continued commitment to finding creative approaches into children's learning and seeking to enable learners to continue along their physical literacy journey in terms of physical competence, knowledge, understanding, confidence, motivation and ability to develop an active and health-promoting lifestyle. In Key Stage 2 they extend their movement vocabulary, movement memory and movement quality, increase manipulative skill ability in a wide range of games equipment, adapt the learning environment to facilitate the playing of many types of cooperative and competitive games and understand how to transfer knowledge of games playing from one situation to another and to create their own games.

A key objective is that learners should transfer to Key Stage 3 with an extensive repertoire of games, with a bank of skills and techniques to develop further as they mature, with strategies and tactics for successful games playing and the determination to meet new challenges and to succeed.

FURTHER READING

Den Duyn, N. (1997) *Game Sense: Developing Thinking Players Workbook*, Canberra: Australian Sports Commission.

Griggs, G. (2007) *Physical Education: The Essential Toolkit for Primary School Teachers*, Blackburn: ePrint.

Light, R. (2013) *Game Sense*, Abingdon: Routledge.

Visual Learning Company (2007) *Invasion Games*, DVD, info@visuallearning.co.uk.

Visual Learning Company (2007) *Net/Wall, Striking/Fielding Games*, DVD, www.visuallearning.co.uk.

CREATIVE PLACES

OUTDOOR AND ADVENTUROUS ACTIVITIES

INTRODUCTION

The *Education Outside the Classroom Manifesto* was published in 2006 by the Department for Education and Skills, after consultation. The aim of the manifesto was to provide all children and young people with a variety of high-quality experiences outside the classroom: 'The world beyond the classroom can stimulate, motivate and bring learning to life' (DfES 2006: 2). Outdoor and adventurous activities were part of the National Curriculum (DfE 2011) at Key Stage 2, where the breadth of study stated that pupils should:

> take part in outdoor activity challenges, including following trails, in familiar, unfamiliar and changing environments, use of a range of orienteering and problem-solving skills, work with others to meet challenges.

In the new National Curriculum (2014), it states that at Key Stage 1, 'pupils should be able to engage in ... cooperative physical activities, in a range of increasingly challenging situations ... developing balance, agility and coordination, and begin to apply these in a range of activities'. It also states that 'pupils should take part in outdoor and adventurous activity, challenges both individually and within a team'. Thomas and Thompson (2004) strongly suggest that every child should be entitled to outdoor learning; however, they suggest that opportunities for outdoor learning have decreased for several reasons, including health and safety concerns, a lack of funding and pressures to meet curriculum targets. Furthermore, *The Campaign for Adventure* (Lewis 2005) is concerned about the current climate of risk aversion, and advocates seeing the positive side of risk (e.g. when children test their skills and learn to face new challenges). Tim Gill (2010: 1–2) argues that:

> Children and young people have a thirst for adventure and challenge. This is evident from their earliest efforts to crawl and walk, and can be seen throughout childhood. What is more, the majority of children grow up to be competent, confident people who lead healthy, fulfilled lives. Despite this, children and young people face growing

adult anxiety over their safety, across many aspects of their everyday lives. While we do not want children to come to harm, our fears can lead us to underestimate their own abilities and to overreact to extremely rare tragedies. Gill (2010) calls for a more balanced approach: an approach that accepts that a degree of risk – properly managed – is not only inevitable, but positively desirable.

When planning and developing creative outdoor and adventurous Physical Education activities, it is important to consider risk benefit. Risk benefit assessment begins with assessing the benefits or objectives of an activity. It then considers the potential risks. This holistic approach enables teachers to view education as not just about delivering a curriculum, but about giving learners:

> the chance to extend their life skills . . . It is about fostering their resilience and sense of responsibility . . . it is about the enjoyment, engagement and excitement of venturing out into the real world, with all its capacity for uncertainty, surprise, stimulation and delight.
>
> (Gill 2010: 22)

Outdoor learning values active, direct experiences in a natural environment, where participants can see, hear, smell and touch in the moment where actions can have real results and consequences:

> There is no limit to the experiences and curiosities that outdoor environments and activities can arouse. Participants frequently discover potential abilities and interests that surprise themselves and others. Safety codes provide clear boundaries and learning goals give clear direction.
>
> (2012, www.englishoutdoorcouncil.org)

An important aspect of creativity is pushing boundaries, so it is important that we challenge and support learners here. 'Life is full of risk so the best way to prepare children for life is to ensure that they understand how to judge risk for themselves' (Danks and Schofield 2006: 15). In this chapter, we consider ways of using outdoor, natural environments to develop social aspects of learning in Physical Education, such as listening, trust, cooperation, teamwork, decision-making, problem-solving, and taking and manage risks. We have chosen two outdoor, natural environments to explore as creative places: the forest and the beach. There is also a brief overview of the swimming pool as another creative place. We argue that it is possible to use Physical Education holistically, and that these inspiring environments are creative places to teach more integrated aspects of Physical Education and to enable learners to apply their knowledge, skills and understanding. The POWER principles are again pertinent here. Learners can experience Physical Education in a range of places where they can see similar and different *purposes* and practice. The use of forest, beach and swimming pool environments enable learners to make connections to previous learning, and use and apply this in a new context. There are a plethora of *opportunities* for all aspects of Physical Education in these creative spaces – this chapter relates many cross-curricular opportunities, and shows how the areas of learning in Physical Education of dance, gymnastics, games, outdoor and adventurous, athletics and swimming can come together. Such places engage learners in considering their own *well-being* and appropriate risk, risk benefit and ways of meeting challenges. These *environments* are rigorous and motivating. Learners can take on a range of roles and investigate, problem-solve, risk-take and have fun, thus revelling in success.

KEY ASPECTS

Forest schools

Forest schools are based on a Scandinavian idea that values children's contact with nature. They were developed in Scandinavia in the 1950s, and stemmed from Early Years Education 'småbørnspædagogik'. This became part of the Danish Early Years programme in the 1980s. Forest schools have been developing in Britain since the 1990s, where there are at least 150, with children of different ages, stages and abilities. Denmark has a similar climate to ours in the UK, and it is becoming increasingly recognised that this 'outdoor' approach to play and learning can have a huge impact on the development of children (Kaplan and Kaplan 1989; Massey 2004; Davis and Waite 2005). For example, research from America (Taylor *et al.* 1998; Fjortoft 2004) found that children who play in natural environments undertake more diverse, creative and imaginative play, forming an important part of a child's development. Forest schools have been defined by the Forest School England network as 'an inspirational process that offers children, young people and adults regular opportunities to achieve, and develop confidence and self-esteem through hands-on learning experiences in a woodland environment' (Forest Education Initiative 2005, www.forest education.org). Some forest schools are privately run, some are supported by local education authorities (LEAs) and some are part of the Forest Education Initiative (FEI), which was set up in 1992 as a partnership between the Forestry Commission, the Tree Council, the Woodland Trust, the British Trust for Conservation Volunteers, Groundwork, the Confederation of Forest Industries (UK) Ltd (ConFor), Community Forests, the Field Studies Council, and the Timber Trade Federation (O'Brien and Murray 2006: 7).

The key features of a forest school are:

- the use of a woodland setting;
- a high ratio of adults to pupils – groups are small, with approximately 10–12 children (this enables the children to play and undertake tasks that challenge them, but also enables appropriate support, as necessary);
- learning linked to the National Curriculum or Foundation Stage objectives;
- freedom for learners to explore using multiple senses – this encourages creative, diverse and imaginative play; and
- regular contact for the children with forest school over a significant period of time includes all year round and all weathers; however, there does need to be a clear set of safety routines and boundaries that enable learners 'to develop a responsible attitude to risk while becoming familiar and confident enough to interact with an ever-changing natural environment' (O'Brien and Murray 2006: 6).

A significant benefit of forest school is the opportunities it presents for the develop-ment of physical knowledge, skills and understanding. This can range from increased stamina to gross and fine motor skills. O'Brien and Murray (2006) document that forest school enables children to enjoy the outdoors and generally be active for the whole session, using their whole body and particular body parts, increasing bone and muscle strength. Forest school offers challenges to physicality as learners negotiate uneven and sometimes rough terrain of different textures. Here, learners are using, improving and increasing motor skills as they are experiencing how to distribute their weight effectively, and make the most of the space available, thereby increasing spatial awareness so as to avoid obstacles, change speed accordingly, and balance and control with greater self-reliance and independence. They are also able to touch and feel the natural materials around them as they climb designated trees, balance on logs, slide on muddy slopes, and dig in the ground. Furthermore, they are also able to play with natural materials such as bracken, twigs, sticks, leaves, stones, earth, cones and seeds, which may be weaved into games or imaginative activities, or used in creating miniature worlds, as well as being able to handle tools, objects and equipment in tasks or activities such as den-building or when making mud pies.

Use of the wood environment

Here follows a range of activities suitable for a variety of ages and stages.

Find someone who? Finding each other/what is the same and what is different?

The children need to move in the space, behind trees, over rocks and so on, and listen carefully for the speaker to speak (the speaker can be a child or an adult). The speaker will say, 'Find someone who . . .'. Then, the speaker chooses what category/who to search for, such as:

> 'Find someone who has the same colour of eyes as you.'
> 'Find someone who likes dancing.'
> 'Find someone who has a pet.'
> 'Find someone who likes carrots.'
> 'Find someone who was born in the same month as you.'

Trust activities

Blindfold and forest trail: Working in pairs, one person is blindfolded and is directed around a forest trail by the other's voice commands, then vice versa. Learners must give short, succinct and accurate instructions using directional language such as left, right, forward, turn and stop. If adding obstacles to negotiate, then add further key words such as step, over, bend and so on.

Contact points: Learners must work with a partner and find connections – this could be initially just eye contact, then fingers, hands, wrists, elbows, arms, shoulders, backs and so on. How many contact points can they find?

Leading and following: In pairs, one person leads and another person follows – this could be an on-the-spot or travelling activity.

What did you say?

In pairs, learners must collect some items together such as bracken, twigs, sticks, leaves, stones, earth, cones and/or seeds. Two of each item must be sought. The amount and variety of items will depend on how complicated the task is to be. Sitting back to back, one person must arrange some items (three or four) in a particular order, and the other person must ask questions in order to replicate the order. Description of the feel, shape and size of the item, as well as directional language, can be encouraged, such as above, below, next to, left, right, under, over and so on.

Scavenger hunt

Children have the opportunity to explore the environment and collect a variety of objects based on a particular theme.

Texture scavenge

Learners search for and collect a variety of natural objects with different textures. They could sort them and give each one a label, such as prickly, rough, smooth and so on. Once the objects have been collected, sorted and discussed, children work in small groups. One person has to do an action/movement depicting prickly, smooth, etc., and the rest of the group has to guess the word that he or she is conveying.

Colour trail

Produce a search card with colours listed, and ask the children to look for items to record on the card so that they can discover and collect a variety of colours from the natural world. For example, green may be a blade of grass or a leaf, brown may be a piece of bark, and so on.

'I spy' woodland trail

Again, a search card can be produced for things to spy. This could include a pine cone, types of trees, types of birds and so on.

Leaf identification

The children have a collection of leaves from trees in the forest and have to find the tree that each leaf is from.

Soil painting/mud prints/mud pies and sculptures

Children need wellington boots and wet mud – they need to stamp, stomp and squelch to make sure that the bottom of the wellington boot is covered in mud, then stamp, stomp and squelch on large rolls of wallpaper to make muddy prints. This also works if learners are able/willing to make muddy bare footprints. Different types of containers can be used to make mud pies and develop sculptures. Again, generate descriptive vocabulary as the learners are engaged in the activities, as these can then be used to generate whole-body movement and dance.

Playing in the snow

Snow lends itself to opportunities that enable learners to experience the contrast in the lightness and quietness of falling snow, and the laid snow, which has a packed, heavier quality. Learners can try to move quickly and then slowly through the snow, experiencing and talking about the staccato quality in movement and the weighted movements. Generate descriptive vocabulary such as delicate, crisp, crunchy, soft, squeak, powder, flurry, dusting, blanket, snowfall and snowstorm. Choices of vocabulary that have been generated can be used to generate whole-body movement and dance, such as exploring ideas in relation to fall (snowfall) and contrasting movements between heavy and light.

Sensory walk

The children go on a sensory adventure to explore the natural environment using their different senses.

Things you can do with a stick

▤ **Table 9.1** Things to do with a stick

Make a wand	Make a stick character
Make a picture frame	Invent stick games
Copy the shapes of sticks	Make a broomstick
Make a fairy house, elf castle or mini den	Make stick art
Play tracking with sticks	Find as many different types of stick as possible

A stick 'offers limitless opportunities for outdoor play and adventure and it provides a starting point for an active imagination and the raw material for transformation into almost anything' (Danks and Schofield 2012: back cover). Ask the children to generate a list of how many things they can do with a stick. These can develop fine motor skills in the making and gross motor skills in the adventures that follow (see Table 9.1).

Do also read *Stickman* by Julia Donaldson.

Rainy day adventures

Consider dancing and singing in the rain, and developing a 'Singing in the Rain' sequence where all the children are dressed in wellington boots and wet-weather clothing. Great, splashy jumps in muddy puddles are essential.

Puddle hunt

Engage in finding as many different shapes, sizes and depths of puddles as possible. Other criteria can include amount of splashes possible and muddiness. Generate descriptive vocabulary and movement such as oozing, squelchy, slippery, sloshing and so on.

Orienteering

Using a basic map initially. Children can identify positions and relate a 2D map to the 3D environment they find around them. They can follow simple directions and a short trail. The map and challenges can become more complex, and can include a quest, as necessary.

Bear hunt

The unit of work 'We're Going on a Bear Hunt', which was shared and discussed in Chapter 3, could easily be based in the forest/wood. The children can go on a bear hunt to explore the site and discover where the bear might be.

Physical responses to stories

The physical experiences that can take place in the inspiring forest/wood setting can be used to develop many cross-curricular links (e.g. a focus on traditional tales and stories that are set in a forest/wood can engage learners in multi-sensory exploration of character and plot). Here are some traditional tales and stories that are set, in full or in part, in a wood:

- *Little Red Riding Hood* (traditional)
- *Goldilocks and the Three Bears* (traditional)
- *Winnie the Pooh* by A. A. Milne
- *Where's My Teddy?* by Martin Waddell
- *The Gruffalo* by Julia Donaldson
- *Into the Woods* by Paul Hoppe
- *Guess What I Found in Dragon Wood?* by Timothy Knapman and Gwen Millward
- *Where the Wild Things Are* by Maurice Sendak
- *We're Going on a Bear Hunt* by Michael Rosen and Helen Oxenbury
- *Guess How Much I Love You?* by Sam McBratney and Anita Jeram Walker
- *Owl Babies* by Martin Waddelll
- *I'm as Quick as a Cricket* by Audrey and Don Wood
- *The Animals of Farthing Wood* by Colin Dann
- *Into the Woods* by Chris Wormell
- *Into the Forest* by Anthony Brown
- *Wood Angel* by Erin Bow
- *Jeremiah in Dark Woods* by Janet and Allan Ahlberg
- *Where the Forest Meets the Sea* and *The Hidden Forest* by Jeannie Baker
- *The Foggy, Foggy Forest* by Nick Sharott

Traditional tales such as *Little Red Riding Hood* and *Goldilocks and the Three Bears* tend to have distinctive, predacable and sequential story patterns and narrative structures since they were originally designed to be sufficiently memorable to the teller and accessible to the listener. Traditional tales and a range of other children's texts such as *The Gruffalo* also have repetitive phrases and chants. Initial physical compositions might begin by considering the narrative, pattern and structure of a text. See Table 9.2 for a version of *Little Red Riding Hood*.

▦ **Table 9.2** Narrative structure of *Little Red Riding Hood*

Beginning	Little Red Riding Hood is asked by her mother to visit her poorly Grandma and take a basket of goodies for her. She is warned to stay on the path. She is walking through to the wood on her way to visit her Grandma.
Middle (plot development)	Little Red Riding Hood meets the Big Bad Wolf, who wants her basket of goodies. She tells him she is on her way to visit Grandma. The Big Bad Wolf suggests that Little Red Riding Hood should stray off the path to pick flowers and take the long route to Grandma's house. The Big Bad Wolf heads off to Grandma's house. The Wolf eats Grandma and dresses up as her. When Little Red Riding Hood arrives, the Wolf pretends to be Grandma. Little Red Riding Hood notices the Wolf's big ears, big eyes and, finally, big teeth.
Climax	The Big Bad Wolf tries to eat Little Red Riding Hood.
Conclusion	A woodman is passing by and hears screams. He cuts the Wolf open and saves Grandma. Little Red Riding Hood and Grandma are safe.

Learners could work in pairs to develop a dance composition using a restricted part of the wood setting (e.g. the use of a tree, where they can go under, in, over or through the tree) – one child could be concerned with Little Red Riding Hood's actions, and the other with the Wolf's actions.

Little Red Riding Hood's actions may include:

▦ *walking* through the woods (around the tree) on an imaginary path;
▦ *gesturing* a conversation with the Wolf;
▦ *meandering* through the wood to find flowers, and *bending* down to the forest floor as though to pick flowers;
▦ *skipping* through the forest (around the tree);
▦ *pushing* movements as though opening a door;
▦ *gesturing* the large ears, large eyes and large teeth movements as a question-and-answer duet with the Wolf; and
▦ *gesturing* shock and *rushing* away.

The Wolf's actions may include:

▦ *hiding* behind the tree;
▦ *gesturing* a conversation with Little Red Riding Hood;
▦ *travelling* at a pace to get to Grandma's house (could add skips, jumps and turns here, around the tree);
▦ *bending* and *stretching* as though dressing;
▦ *laying down* or *climbing up* the tree in wait for Little Red Riding Hood;
▦ *gesturing* the response to large ears, large eyes and large teeth movements from Little Red Riding Hood as a question-and-answer duet; and
▦ *sudden movements* trying to *grab* Little Red Riding Hood, but she rushes away.

Older learners could also explore power struggles, alter tales, and subvert, transform and mix by entwining a range of key actions and features. Anthony Browne's *Into the Forest* is a good example to lean on. Further dance work could relate to repetition, motif and development, with three inspired by *Goldilocks and the Three Bears*. There are some dance works that can be viewed for inspiration on YouTube, such as at www.youtube.com/watch?v=6FPaK_JO4ao.

Older learners may draw on myths and legend-based texts, and could create their own physical task-based adventure and narrative, such as 'The Forest of Doom', based on a quest or journey.

Learners could also consider the British wildlife that may live in a wood, such as those featured in stories such as *The Animals of Farthing Wood* and *Guess How Much I Love You?* These texts feature mammals (e.g. mice, rabbits, hares, squirrels, badgers, foxes, moles and hedgehogs), amphibians (e.g. toads and frogs), and birds (e.g. owls and wood pigeons). It may be that the children have seen some of the animals moving in the wood, such as rabbits, squirrels and birds. The qualities and dynamics of the ways that the mammals, amphibians and birds move can be explored, and descriptive vocabulary developed (see Table 9.3).

Rather than a literal interpretation and simply 'being' an animal, the children could choose three of any the words and related dynamics (heavy/light, fast/slow, fluid/staccato) as starting points for development as group pieces of composition. Spatial elements, such as levels, size, on the spot, travelling, directions and pathways, could be developed, as well as a consideration of weight, speed and flow. I recommend *L'enfant et les sortilèges* as an inspirational professional dance work that has a range of animals in it (see www.youtube.com/watch?v=ozIf-d8WarY.

■ **Table 9.3** Examples of qualities and dynamics

scamper	stretch	dart
scurry	curl	sudden
hop	hesitant	twist
bounce	speedy	jerky
curious	hover	leap
shy	swoop	hang
meander	soar	fall
whizz	creep	squiggle

Beach schools

Beach schools, as the name suggests, can take place on any beach, but some are more appropriate than others. Beach schools were developed from the concept of forest schools. Many of the creative, physical activities suggested for forest schools could also be undertaken in a beach school context. However, by the nature of the seaside as a place where land meets water, there are lots of pebbles, shingle and/or sand. There will also be shallow water and rocky areas, potentially including rock pools.

Similar to forest school, the key features of a beach school are:

■ the use of a beach/seaside setting;
■ a high ratio of adults to pupils – groups are small, with approximately 10–12 children (this enables the children to play and undertake tasks that challenge them, but also enables appropriate support as necessary);
■ learning linked to the National Curriculum or Foundation Stage objectives;
■ freedom for learners to explore using multiple senses – this encourages creative, diverse and imaginative play; and
■ regular contact for the children with beach school over a significant period of time includes all year round and all weathers (however, there does need to be a clear set of safety routines and boundaries that enable learners 'to develop a responsible attitude to risk while becoming familiar and confident enough to interact with an ever-changing natural environment') (O'Brien and Murray 2006: 6).

Use of the outdoor beach environment

Moving on sand

If the beach is a sandy one, the children can experience travelling, jumping, turning, rolling, etc. on sand. A discussion can be developed in relation to how and why it is different/difficult to run on sand as opposed to grass, a playground (concrete) or a track.

Exploring stones/pebbles

Learners can undertake supervised throwing of stones/pebbles into the sea. The children can also skim stones/pebbles using flatter shapes. There can be an investigation and search to find the best skimmer, and criteria can relate to weight, shape and distance thrown.

Paddling

Children can paddle in the sea and jump waves as the tide comes in, looking and pre-empting when it is the best time to jump. Perhaps try holding hands with a partner or in groups of three or more. Is this easier or more difficult? Why? Ask the children to articulate if they can feel sand, shingle or pebbles under foot. Can they feel the pull and drag of the sea? Is it sometimes tricky to balance?

Beach scavenger hunt

Talk about all of the elements of nature that the children could find at the shore. This can include seashells, seaweed, dry grass, stones/pebbles and more. Let the children go on a scavenger hunt to find items on a list of things commonly found at the beach, and then bring them back into a group to discuss and observe their findings.

Create a challenge or game

After an initial idea is shared with the children from you as the teacher, groups of children are given a range of equipment, and they need to create a physical challenge or game (rather like the television programme *The Cube*). Equipment can include a variety of balls, including beach balls; a range of containers, such as buckets; and a variety of digging implements, such as spades, hoops and markers. Use of sand and seawater can also be incorporated. As suggested in the National Curriculum, games skills such as travelling with, sending and receiving balls and other equipment in different ways, and tactics for attacking and defending, could be applied. Older children can plan, use and adapt strategies, tactics and compositional ideas for small-group and small-team activities; develop and use their knowledge of the principles behind the strategies, tactics and ideas to improve their effectiveness; and apply rules and conventions for different activities.

Parachute games

Parachute games encourage cooperative, non-competitive play, and reinforce turn-taking and sharing. Here are some examples of parachute games:

All Change: A leader calls out a birthday or a category such as months, numbers or colours. Children swap places under the chute before it falls to earth.

Beach Ball Fun: Use a beach ball, moving it around on the parachute with waves of the parachute.

Cat and Mouse: Everyone holds the parachute so that it is stretched out at about waist height. Someone becomes a mouse and goes underneath. Someone else becomes a cat and goes on top. The rest of the group try to hide the mouse by moving the parachute up and down.

Merry-Go-Round: Turn the body so that the parachute is held with only one hand. Walk, hop, jump and skip around holding the parachute. It looks like a merry-go-round.

Mushroom: The children raise their arms, lifting the parachute over their heads, pulling the parachute behind them and sitting down with their bottoms on the edge of the parachute.

Rollerball: Everyone holds the parachute taut. Place a ball near the edge and try to make the ball roll around the edge of the parachute. The children can try changing the direction or speeding up.

Sharks: Everyone sits on the ground with their legs stretched out under the parachute as the parachute is held at chest height. One or two children crawl around under the parachute and are 'sharks'. They quietly grab the legs of anyone around the perimeter (with many blood-curdling screams), and pull them under the canopy. The shark now swaps places.

Exploring rock pools

Learners may find starfish, limpets, crabs, mussels, barnacles and so on. Encourage the children to work in groups and allocate roles such as photographer.

Examining shells

Collect shells from the beach (or take some with you to the beach). Talk about the shells, look closely at them, describe them and make a record of descriptive vocabulary.

Inspiring gymnastics

The children could try making on-the-spot and travelling actions for the words generated that describe shells, such as smooth and spiky. The children could work individually, and then in pairs, as they curl, stretch, tense and relax the body. Two pairs could be joined where they could choose three words to use to create a sequence. Furthermore, children could develop gymnastic sequences based on shell imagery, which have a clear beginning and end – perhaps a balance, roll and jump. Canon, counterbalance, symmetry and asymmetry could also be incorporated.

Site-specific dance

Learners can use the site of the beach to create site-specific dance (i.e. dance composition that has a relationship with the site and depends on the site for it to be effective). The dance composition may be inspired by, and use:

■ the ebb and flow, tide going in and out, and qualities of the sea;
■ activities that may occur on the beach – fishing, rock pool searching, paddling;
■ movement of seaweed and/or sea creatures;
■ shells;
■ shapes of seaweed;
■ fish fins, scales and tails.

Warm-up and cool-down ideas could include:

■ reaching to the sun;
■ handprints in the sand;
■ making letters with toes in the sand;
■ lying flat and sunbathing;
■ brushing sand off arms and legs;
■ standing and kicking legs in the sea as paddling; and
■ swinging movements as though the tide is coming in and out.

The suggested ideas based on the poem 'At the Sea-Side' in Chapter 4 could also be incorporated.

Build a river

The beach is the ideal setting to teach learners about how water flows naturally to the sea. The children can build mountains in the sand, and then create a gulley that leads to the water. A bucket filled with seawater can be poured gently over the sand mountain, then let the children watch the water stream down the gulley to the sea in the same manner that water flows in streams and rivers to the sea after rain.

Beach athletics

A number of athletic activities and challenges can take place using the sand instead of a school playground or field. These can also be integrated into some of the previous suggested activities (see Table 9.4).

■ **Table 9.4** Examples of athletic challenges

Can you jump from standing?	Can you explore the five different jumps?
Can you jump accurately into a target from standing?	Can you take a running jump?
Can you throw with one hand?	Can you explore the words fling, pull, push and heave when throwing different objects?
Can you throw different objects with one hand?	Can you show two different types of throw?
Can you run very fast on sand?	Can you change speeds when running?
Can you change speed and direction when running?	Can you run at the correct speed for the distance?

Leaning on literature

As in the use of the forest/wood setting, physical experiences that can take place in the inspiring beach setting can be used to develop many cross-curricular links. A focus on stories, for example, that make connections to a seaside setting can come to life as the children engage with them while in the setting. Here are some useful stories:

- *The Snail and the Whale* by Julia Donaldson
- *Tiddler* by Julia Donaldson
- *On My Beach There Are Many Pebbles* by Leo Lionni
- *If You Find a Rock* by Peggy Christian and Barbara Hirsch Lember
- *Hooray for Fish* by Lucy Cousins
- *The Rainbow Fish* by Marcus Pfister
- *Where the Forest Meets the Sea* and *The Hidden Forest* by Jeannie Baker

Swimming pools

Just a little about swimming pools – a swimming pool can be a very creative place. Developing water confidence with a range of props and activities can be motivating for learners as they feel their bodies in water and develop body confidence in water. It is paramount that safety is the top priority – small groups with plenty of adults, and never turn your back on a beginner. There are a number of challenges for older children. The 2014 National Curriculum states that 'all schools must provide swimming instruction either in Key Stage 1 or Key Stage 2'. Here are a number of activities that focus on water confidence.

Nursery rhymes and songs

Early work can develop with action songs and rhymes, and using water to splish and splash the actions.

Underwater signals

Ideally, the earlier in a child's development, the better, regarding going under the water. A signal 'ready, [child's name], and go' can be helpful so the child can get ready by holding his or her breath and going under, and then pushing him or herself back up above the water straight away.

Safe entry into water and jumping in

Various different ways of entering the water can be tried, and then submersion and different types of jumps can be tried – who can make a big splash?

Props

▨ **Table 9.5** Examples of props for water confidence and play

Kickboards	Seal flip rings
Floats	Pool sticks, dive rings
Super soakers	Squinters
Pool Frisbee	Nets
Large hoops	Noodles
Various plastic balls	Various inflatables

The above props in Table 9.5 can be used in many different ways with an emphasis on developing water confidence and play. See how many activities and games you and your learners can develop.

Leaning on literature

All the texts mentioned for the beach school can be incorporated into swimming pool play.

Use of imagery

This is purposeful as it aids children's ability to make connections to other experiences such as 'hold your noodle like a steering wheel', and 'dive like a dolphin'.

Body readiness

Lots of play involving stretching legs, splashing, splashy toes, making body long and laying flat, doggy paddle, stretching arms, pushing off, turning in water, floating like a starfish and so on will aid learners in developing skills that they will need when learning strokes.

Sculling and treading water

Lots of play and 'chase' types games, as well as obstacles and treasure hunts, can be developed.

Shipwreak

Here, children can use their imagination and develop numerous adventures and rescues. It is important that such activities are supervised.

Swimming strokes

For information on teaching swimming strokes and distance swimming, please see www.swimming.org.

SUMMARY

The use of the natural environments of the forest and the beach can inspire and motivate learners physically, socially, emotionally and cognitively. Learners can develop greater confidence, social skills, vocabulary, knowledge and understanding, communication, and concentration. Furthermore, such physical and creative opportunities enable learners to develop greater self-awareness, self-regulation, and ability to weigh up risk and stay safe. They display intrinsic motivation, empathy and independence, and can recognise that different tasks affect the body in different ways.

FURTHER READING

Barton, B. (2006) *Safety, Risk and Adventure in Outdoor Activities*, London: Sage.

Danks, F. (2009) *Go Wild! 101 Things to Do Outdoors Before You Grow Up*, London: Francis Lincoln.

Danks, F. and Schofield, J. (2012) *The Stick Book: Loads of Things You Can Make or Do with a Stick*, London: Francis Lincoln.

Danks, F. and Schofield, J. (2013) *The Wild Weather Book: Loads of Things to Do Outdoors in Rain, Wind and Snow*, London: Francis Lincoln.

CHAPTER

10

THE CREATIVE PRACTITIONER

PLANNING FOR CREATIVE PHYSICAL EDUCATION

INTRODUCTION

Teachers are paramount in creating creative teaching and learning opportunities. This can only happen due to the creative practitioner's passion, commitment and engagement. A belief in the value of teaching Physical Education and creative teaching will enable approaches to teaching Physical Education that value exploration; inspire, challenge and lean on learners' interests, enthusiasms and thirst for wanting to know more; and, in turn, this enables learners to become more physically literate. In this chapter, we discuss planning for creative Physical Education, where we argue that planning is underpinned by our understanding of learning theories, values, beliefs, teaching styles and strategies. We also give an overview of pragmatics such as differentiation, safe practice, long-, medium- and short-term planning, aims, objectives/outcomes, and assessment. In addition, we explore ways of using technology to enhance teaching Physical Education creatively. The last part of this chapter returns to the introduction to this book, and argues for the POWER principles and the importance of keeping abreast of current thinking, especially if you are in role as a subject leader/coordinator. Finally, we remind ourselves of the connection to physical literacy as a holistic approach to Physical Education.

KEY ASPECTS

Planning for creative Physical Education

Alexander (2004: 11) states that pedagogy is 'morally purposeful activity, of which teaching is a part, which we call education'. He advocates the importance of knowing the wider culture (the philosophy, history, literature and art of the country), of child development and children's learning (psychology, physiology, etc.), and of subject knowledge as ways of understanding this 'purposeful activity'. Successful planning is a way to provide high-quality creative Physical Education. Planning is underpinned by an understanding about pedagogy and how learning happens (e.g. behavioural, cognitive, social, experiential) (Sanders 2012). This book advocates an active, creative approach to developing learning.

The content is informed by underpinning learning theories, values, beliefs, teaching styles and strategies; these are all influenced by our commitment to a creative approach. The influential learning theories are drawn from Vygotsky (1978), who emphasised social engagement and the effectiveness of the 'more knowledgeable other' as facilitator, and Bruner (1966), who examined modes of representation of information. The provision of support/guidance and challenge or scaffolding (Bruner 1966; Vygotsky 1978) and experiential learning theories (Jarvis *et al.* 2005) that value the whole person – cognitive, physical, emotional and spiritual – are also key. Such values and beliefs will inform our choices of teaching styles as the methods we choose to teach, and teaching strategies (open questions, use of imagery, demonstration and modelling) as the manner in which we enhance teaching. Teaching styles have been considered by Mosston and Ashworth (2002), and Hayden-Davies and Whitehead (2010) have expanded upon their work to describe teacher and learner roles (see Table 10.1).

Particular choices of teaching styles that acknowledge 'teaching for creativity', as well as 'teaching creatively' (NACCCE 1999: 29), such as guided discovery (divergent) and a *scaffolded* approach, can be particularly helpful in encouraging learner independence. In turn, such strategies lend themselves to greater creative responses from learners.

■ **Table 10.1** Teaching styles

Teaching Style	Teacher and Learner Roles
Command/didactic	Teacher as instructor makes all the decisions, learner copies and is mainly passive
Practice	Teacher prescribes and gives feedback and encouragement, learner rehearses, repeats and improves
Guided discovery (convergent)	Teacher guides and sets tasks building on what children know, can do and understand, learners investigate to find a solution
Guided discovery (divergent)	Teacher prompts and sets tasks building on what children know, can do and understand, learners creatively investigate to find various solutions
Reciprocal	Teacher gives guidelines to learners who work in pairs and give feedback to peers
Learner-designed/participant-led	Teacher enables and advises learners how to lead, learners initiate
Self-check	Learners evaluate their own performance in collaboration with the teacher who acts as a mentor
Inclusion	Learners select from a variety of tasks based on their ability/requirements facilitated by the teacher

Differentiation

This book has offered many practical suggestions for teaching Physical Education creatively, but these may need to be adapted to suit your learners. Differentiation provides individual and appropriate ways of achieving learning for each learner. Ways of differentiating are often by outcome, where the same task is set for all but is purposely open-ended, and can be interpreted in various ways to enable learners to respond differently and produce a range of outcomes. Or differentiation is by task, where tasks and activities may be set at different levels, with differing expectations.

The STEP approach is useful here (www.youthsporttrust.org) for planning for differentiation:

■ Support – offering varying levels of support, challenge and independence.
■ Task – setting various tasks or activities.
■ Equipment – using different sizes, shapes, or types of equipment or resources.
■ Pace – varying times that it may take individuals to complete tasks or activities.

A consideration of these areas will aid inclusive approaches to teaching.

Safe practice

Ensuring that Physical Education experiences are physically and emotionally safe (Whitlam 2012) relates to being mindful of appropriateness, which was an area that was discussed in Chapter 9. This includes:

Clothing

■ Long hair should be tied back.
■ Jewellery should not be worn.
■ Footwear should be appropriate to the activity, floor surface and space.
■ Floor should be clean and safe, particularly if learners have bare feet.

Behaviour

■ Emphasising spatial awareness and positive use of space, and relationship building.
■ Ideally, a consensus of acceptable behaviour and the use of constructive language in a culture of responsibility for the physical and psychological well-being of others should be developed.

Physical development and well-being

■ Knowledge and understanding of how children within the primary phase 4–11 years grow, develop and change physically and emotionally is important when planning, teaching and assessing. Furthermore, applied knowledge and understanding of how the children you are working with (your class), as a class and as individuals, grow, develop, change, think and feel is essential in order that all are able to fully engage with Physical Education creatively.
■ Promoting a responsible attitude to health.
■ Developing an environment that is respectful, encouraging, supportive and that values well-being.

Good practice

■ Provide warm-up and cool-down activities that prepare learners physically and psychologically.
■ Expect safe use of props and equipment.
■ Promote safe execution of movement.

Spaces

■ Ensure learners are thoroughly warmed up if using a cold, inside space.
■ Avoid high-impact work, such as jumps and falls to the floor, if using a hard floor.
■ Free of unnecessary obstacles.
■ Always have a first-aid kit available.
■ If outside, wear suitable clothing for the conditions.
■ Avoid going near trees in thunderstorms or very strong winds.
■ Never go on icy ponds or rivers.
■ Always wash hands after playing in mud.
■ See also Whitlam (2012).

The language of planning

You may well be an experienced practitioner who is very familiar with these terms, but for those new to teaching, it is worthwhile being clear with the language of planning.

Scheme of work

A scheme of work is the long-term plan that relates to a particular context, age/stage of learners, and the space, time, resources, aims and objectives/outcomes.

Unit of work

This is a medium-term block of work (often around half a term) that identifies a particular area of learning and theme (such as gymnastics and balancing), learning objectives/ outcomes, age/stage development, activities that account for continuity and progression, and resources. Cross-curricular links can be made here and/or a more holistic way of working, such as those suggested in Chapter 9 and the use of forest school. Cross-curricular links can be made in different ways. The dimension(s) can be:

■ taught through subjects, with links across subjects being made where these links are relevant and authentic and contribute to a richer, broader learning experience for young people;
■ the focus of timetabled thematic days, activity weeks or events;
■ integrated into the events of the school (e.g. running mini-enterprises, organising fundraising events or performing at celebration events within and beyond school);
■ a focus for educational visits and out-of-school learning; and
■ introduced through visiting experts who are able to stimulate discussion and debate around the dimension(s).

(DCSF 2008: 1)

Session plan

This is the outline structure that takes each session from the unit of work and breaks it down in a linear way. For example, a way of working in dance could have the following structure:

■ warm up;
■ introducing/building on a dance theme/idea/stimulus;
■ creative movement opportunities (exploration);
■ development of movement material (investigation and problem-solving);
■ selection/rejection/refinement (decision-making);
■ performance opportunities;
■ appreciation opportunities; and
■ cool down.

Aims

An aim is the driving force behind the work, often a longer term-goal, and demonstrates what you want learners to know, do and understand by the end of a longer plan. It is worth considering the *depth-first* or *breadth-first* approach:

A purely logical development may not always be the best pedagogic approach . . . depth-first [approach is where] a particular topic is explored in detail before moving on to the next one, and a breadth first in which a topic is taken only as far as is needed to be used in other topics.

(Avis *et al.* 2010: 136)

Tomkins (2012) relates this to teaching a sequence; one approach is to show 'the whole sequence with the learners observing and "having a go" (breadth approach) or break the sequence down and explore all aspects of each section in terms of space, weight, time (depth approach) before performing the whole sequence'.

Objectives/outcomes

Objectives are 'the driving force behind what you teach, how you teach it and what you assess' (Tomkins 2012: 70). Thinking progressively is useful here in the development of knowledge, skills and understanding, and drawing on Bloom's six types of thinking can be helpful in constructing objectives/outcomes that are measurable/can be assessed (see Table 10.2).

Assessment

Assessment enables us to see whether our planning and content are appropriate and support learning. It may be that you are concerned with how learners are using the body with increasing confidence, coordination, control and creativity, and how they are applying skills such as controlled landings in jumps or evaluating strengths in a gymnastic sequence. The basis of effective assessment is having a clear view of what learners can learn during the session (objectives/outcomes). Observation of learners' responses instigates appropriate

■ **Table 10.2** Bloom's six types of thinking

	Knowledge	Comprehension	Application	Analysis	Synthesis	Evaluation
Key Words	Know Describe	Understand Explain Describe	Demonstrate Use	Examine Analyse	Compose Create	Critique Judge
Descriptors	Fact-based: Who What When Where	Recognise Identify	Explaining Showing Demonstrating	Categorise Identify Describe	Combining Composing Creating	Judge Merit Quality
Process	Recalling Remembering	Grasping the meaning of material (i.e. different levels)	Applying knowing and doing	Breaking down material	Putting material together to form a new creation	Judging Merit Critiquing
Verbs	List Name Observe Memorise Remember Recall	Identify Summarise Describe	Explain Apply Show Use Sequence Organise Imagine	Characterise Categorise Examine Distinguish between Describe Analyse	Create Relate Invent Plan Compose Construct Design Improve Edit	Evaluate Critique Judge Value Decide Conclude

feedback, as support and challenge can be offered immediately, and this can be done informally throughout the session; this is therefore assessment for learning. In addition, this information can be used to build into the next session and inform future planning. For example, in an observation, you may focus on:

■ phrases of movement – preparation, execution and development such as in an over arm throw, a combination of movement in a gymnastic sequence, or how pairs interact together;

■ general to specific – an overall impression of movement quality, and then look at specific body parts and so on (e.g. when observing running, we may look at the whole action, arm action, leg action, and trunk and head, or the use of space in a dance); and

■ physical literacy – see earlier chapters for more information on this important concept: motivation, confidence, physical competence (understanding and knowledge should feature in the *experience* of physical literacy).

Technology

Of course, Physical Education is about being physically active, but there are ways that technology can be used to enhance the teaching of Physical Education creatively. Primary-aged learners are immersed in technology from birth, and are 'digital natives' (Prensky 2001), so they are very used to handling remote controls, game consoles and controls, MP3 players, tablets, and smartphones, for example. ICT offers a range of tools so that pupils can analyse, evaluate and compare performance. This includes:

▨ using performance analysis software and hardware;
▨ using ICT to record and analyse performance;
▨ using ICT to track participation, involvement and improvement in physical activity; and
▨ creating multimedia films and productions in conjunction with other curriculum areas.

Furthermore, learners can:

▨ access, select and interpret information;
▨ recognise patterns, relationships and behaviours;
▨ model, predict and hypothesise;
▨ test reliability and accuracy;
▨ review and modify their work to improve the quality;
▨ communicate with others and present information;
▨ evaluate their work;
▨ improve efficiency;
▨ be creative and take risks; and
▨ gain confidence and independence.

(Becta 2009: 2)

Standard software can provide plenty of opportunities, such as using spreadsheets, presentation programs and different ways of analysing data. Pedometers count and monitor the number of steps taken throughout the day. Most pedometers provide a fairly accurate count of steps taken during ambulatory activities such as walking, jogging and running. Learners can predict and investigate the amount of steps taken during a particular activity. These could also be incorporated into creative space activities at a forest or beach school, as in Chapter 9. You can also download full lesson plans at www.pecentral.org/lessonideas/pedometer/pedometerlessonindex.htm for using pedometers.

Technology can bring accessibility – bringing the world to the classroom. For example, the use of television and the Internet can be used to immerse children in the culture of sport and dance by using excerpts of televised events such as the Olympics and Wimbledon, as well as use of the plethora of professional dance works (theatre-style, installation, site-specific and those using digital images), which can be used to inspire, challenge and support learners in developing their own ideas. Interactive whiteboards (large, touch-sensitive boards that control a computer connected to a digital projector) are particularly useful for multimedia/multimodal presentation. Use of film and animation can provide engaging stimulus for developing movement language. Use of digital/video cameras for capturing work in progress and movement to memory can be useful for teacher assessment, where you may look at preparation, execution and follow-through of movements such as in a jump, but children can also do the filming and analysis themselves. If using a digital camera, the pictures/images are stored in computer memory and can be displayed directly onto a computer monitor or imported into a graphics/art package or basic editing computer program so that children are able to make their own Physical Education films. 2D and 3D animation programs can be used to create short cartoons or films. Software such as Dartfish (video analysis), Observing Children Moving (a set of multimedia resources) and Isadora (real-time media manipulation software that can create interactive visuals, sounds and environments) can be useful.

Global Positioning System (GPS) uses 24 satellites and ground stations as reference points to calculate geographic locations and accurately track a specific activity. For example, using a portable GPS unit could provide information about distance and time between two points of travel, so again could be incorporated into outdoor environments such as getting to forest school, beach school and back to the school playground. Stopwatches could also be incorporated here. As small receivers become more affordable and accessible to the general public (e.g. in laptop computers and mobile telephones), GPS may be more widely used to assess and promote physical activity. The use of websites and interactive games as 'exertainment' such as *Wii Sports* and various dance mats may be useful as a small part of a wider Physical Education offer, but should not be the only Physical Education offered. However, children can investigative such physical activities where learners access, select and interpret information, predict and hypothesise and review and modify their work to improve the quality.

The POWER principles

We argue in this book that Physical Education has the potential to bring the learner body confidence and power. We use the notion of power as we advocate the POWER principles, which you will have met in each chapter:

■ **PURPOSE** – Valuing purposeful physical exploration and meaning-making.
■ **OPPORTUNITIES** – Harnessing opportunities within and across the curriculum.
■ **WELL-BEING** – Developing awareness of health and well-being.
■ **ENVIRONMENT** – Providing a motivating and inclusive climate.
■ **REVEL** – Initiating celebration of physical success, achievement and progression.

These principles are also informed by pedagogy: learning theories, styles and strategies. For us, these principles have longevity in relation to developing content and approaches to teaching, and support the notion that teaching is an emotional as well as a cerebral activity (Hargreaves 2001). Teaching Physical Education creatively is experiential learning, and therefore relates to the idea that we are working with the whole person: 'the cognitive, the physical, the emotional and the spiritual: that is, the individual's knowledge, skills, attitudes, values, beliefs, emotions and senses' (Jarvis *et al.* 2005: 55). The importance of the social and cultural context in which people demonstrate creativity must also be considered, as creativity involves being in relationship with oneself, other people, significant others and with Physical Education. Feldman *et al.* (1994) contend that creativity arises from the interaction between the 'intelligence' of individuals, 'the areas of human endeavour, disciplines, crafts or pursuits, and the field, such as people, institutions, award mechanisms and 'knowledgeable others' through which judgements of individual performances in society are made' (Loveless 2002: 10).

At present, we seem to be living in a fast-paced 'knowledge age', and the danger is that due to pressure on practitioners to act in a didactic way, to tell children, as passive rather than active learners, as much knowledge as possible. In this way there becomes a superficial skill base and knowledge and understanding of the world for learners. Primary-aged children *must* move; they must be given opportunities for reflection, to develop resourcefulness and resilience (Claxton 2000), to make sense of knowledge, to play, investigate and push the boundaries of their bodies – this is how children use and apply the knowledge and skills. Governments and their related curriculum documentation will come and go, but the POWER principles *are* what Physical Education is about – these stay as solid foundations from which to build.

The creative practitioner

A number of characteristics that constitute a creative practitioner/individual have been suggested:

■ openness to experiences;
■ independence/ self-reliance;
■ confidence;
■ willingness to take risks;
■ a sense of humour or playfulness;
■ enjoyment of experimentation;
■ sensitivity;
■ lack of feeling of being threatened;
■ personal courage;
■ unconventionality;
■ flexibility; and
■ persistence.

(Shallcross, cited in Craft 2000: 13)

In addition, Sternberg and Lubart's (1999) 'confluence model' is useful. Here, six resources converge:

1 intellectual abilities;
2 knowledge;
3 styles of thinking;
4 personality;
5 motivation; and
6 environment.

Mikhail Csikszentmihalyi (1996) identifies a common characteristic of creative people as 'flow'. This is an automatic, effortless and yet highly focused state of consciousness when engaged in often difficult/challenging activities, which stretch a person's capacity, while involving an element of novelty or discovery. He elaborates the description of 'flow' through identifying nine elements that such activity provides:

1 clear goals;
2 immediate feedback;
3 balance between challenges and skills;
4 merging of action and awareness;

5   elimination of distractions;
6   lack of fear of failure;
7   lack of self-consciousness;
8   distortion of sense of time; and
9   autotelic activity (enjoyment for its own sake).

Furthermore, Loveless (2002: 9) argues that 'individual states of intuition, reverie, even boredom play a role in creativity and problem-solving'. Studies have indicated how creativity is enhanced in a state of reverie and imagery (Lynn and Rhue 1986; Claxton 1999, 2000):

> Such states are not just 'letting it flow' or 'leaving it to luck', but acknowledging a way of knowing which is not necessarily conscious and draws upon resources of knowledge, skill and experience in order to make new combinations, explorations and transformations.
>
> (Boden 2001: 9)

Of course, we are not suggesting that the practitioner uses the research findings above as checklists to identify whether he or she is indeed a creative practitioner, but such findings can inform reflection and practice – how do we develop the most powerful creative environment? The POWER principles relate to effective pedagogy, provision and practice – the creative practitioner who values and profiles purpose, relevance, children's interests, physical development, emotional development, well-being, ideas development, flexibility, physical exploration, play, investigation, collaboration, risk-taking, appropriate risk/risk benefit, and meaning-making in their planning, provision and practice is a high-quality and creative practitioner.

We argued in Chapter 1 that practitioners and children need to be confident to be creative risk-takers, and that this means adopting a 'creative state of mind' (Barnes 2007: 137), or, as Galton (2008: xi) found, 'creative practitioners appeared to equate creativity with "flexibility of the mind"'. The creative practitioner is mindful of keeping abreast of current thinking, which may be the latest prescribed curriculum or research report. Importantly, however, this is seen with a critical eye, in relation to pedagogical understanding and principles that underpin approaches to, and content of, teaching and learning. The creative practitioner finds ways to fit the curriculum requirements to his or her principles and pedagogy, rather than the principles and pedagogy fitting into the curriculum content. In this way, the curriculum requirements and content do not need to be viewed as a constraint to creativity, opportunities or possibilities.

Keeping abreast of current thinking

It may be that you are engaged in developing Physical Education as a whole school, perhaps as a subject leader/coordinator. The Physical Education leader is a role model, so will endeavour to fuel the enthusiasm and creativity of others, as well as being involved in, for example:

■   being aware of national and local developments in Physical Education;
■   supporting colleagues in all aspects of the Physical Education curriculum;

- reviewing the school policy and schemes of work, including regular monitoring and evaluation of content and methodology;
- encouraging and supporting staff in the implementation of the policy and monitoring the consistency and progression through the Key Stages;
- supporting short-term planning for each group;
- purchasing and organising Physical Education resources and ensuring they are readily available and well maintained;
- encouraging and organising professional development opportunities, as appropriate; and
- supporting the running of out-of-school events and activities.

At the end of this chapter, there is a list useful websites that can offer a wealth of information, ideas and developments.

PHYSICAL LITERACY

If we agree that teaching Physical Education creatively enables 'motivation, confidence, physical competence, knowledge and understanding to value and take responsibility for maintaining purposeful physical pursuits throughout the lifecourse', then we are aiming to develop learners who are physically literate. In further detail:

- Physical literacy can be described as a disposition characterised by the motivation and confidence to capitalise on innate movement/physical potential to make a significant contribution to the quality of life.
- Individuals who are physically literate will move with poise, economy and confidence in a wide variety of physically challenging situations.
- Physically literate individuals will be perceptive in 'reading' all aspects of the physical environment, anticipating movement needs or possibilities and responding appropriately to these, with intelligence and imagination.
- These individuals will have a well-established sense of self as embodied in the world. This, together with an articulate interaction with the environment, will engender positive self-esteem and self-confidence.
- Sensitivity to and awareness of embodied capability will lead to fluent self-expression through non-verbal communication and to perceptive and empathetic interaction with others.
- In addition, physically literate individuals will have the ability to identify and articulate the essential qualities that influence the effectiveness of their own movement performance, and have an understanding of the principles of embodied health, with respect to basic aspects such as exercise, sleep and nutrition.

(Whitehead 2009; www.physical-literacy.org.uk)

Let us return again to the chart (Figure 10.1, and see Maude, Chapter 2) that makes connections between physical literacy and creativity, and raises movement, effective engagement and environmental aspects as significant. Teaching Physical Education creatively will motivate and engage children, who will develop technically in terms of skills, but will also be able to apply knowledge, skills and understanding imaginatively, creatively and in a range of contexts.

Contributions of Creativity to Enhancing Physical Literacy	Attributes of Physical Literacy	Contributions of Physical Literacy to Enhancing Creativity
⟹	⟸ ⟹	⟸
	Movement Attributes	
Through tackling self-set as well as teacher-promoted creative challenges, learners can explore alternative aspects of movement vocabulary, enhance and evaluate creative experiences and thereby also gain further knowledge and understanding of physical competence	Physical Competence Knowledge Understanding	Increasing movement vocabulary and enhancing skilful performance can expand potential for creative activity Through movement observation, analysis of self and others and through the study of movement, learners can bring greater knowledge to their creative endeavours
	Affective Attributes	
Enabling creative learners to enhance their confidence, motivation and self-esteem through encouraging and supporting their playfulness, inquisitiveness, creative enquiry, experimentation, searching, failing and succeeding, provides increased depth to physical literacy	Confidence Motivation Self-esteem	Building increasing confidence engendered through skilful performance and familiarity with wide applications of movement, enhances intrinsic motivation and self-esteem generated through achievement and success
	Interactive Attributes	
Creative exploration of movement spaces, the texture of the environment, work surfaces and access to various levels, pathways, and directions of movement, enhances learners' physical literacy	Environments – indoor and outdoor	Skilful exploration of a wide range of environments enables learners to apply related experience from one environment to another, thereby extending opportunities for the flowering of creativity
Working creatively alongside younger learners and peers as well as with older children and adults strengthens the ability to engage in social aspects of physical literacy, such as cooperation and competition	People	Interacting comfortably in movement with younger learners and peers as well as with older children and adults can stimulate and strengthen the creative the experience
Free, creative movement exploration of natural resources, man-made and manufactured equipment promotes extensive variety, proficiency and enrichment in the experience and management of resources and equipment	Resources	Having the ability to interact with a wide range of natural, man-made and manufactured resources, increases exploratory and creative opportunities

▨ **Figure 10.1** Relationships between physical literacy and creativity

SUMMARY

In this chapter, we have examined the importance of pedagogy and practical considerations in planning for creative Physical Education. We have also argued for the POWER principles, raised the importance of keeping abreast of current thinking and related our creative approach to the holistic notion of physical literacy. We hope you enjoy *Teaching Physical Education Creatively*.

FURTHER READING

National Curriculum
www.qcda.gov.uk

National Organisations
Active Places – www.activeplaces.com
Arts Council England – www.artscouncil.org.uk
Association for Physical Education – www.afpe.org.uk
British Gymnastics – www.british-gymnastics.co.uk
British Olympic Association – www.boa.org.uk
Department for Culture, Media and Sport – www.culture.gov.uk
Department for Education – www.education.gov.uk
Department for Children, Schools and Families – www.dcsf.gov.uk
English Folk Dance and Song Society – www.efdss.org
International Physical Literacy Association (IPLA) – www.physical-literacy.org.uk
National Dance Teachers Association – www.ndta.org.uk
Ofsted – www.ofsted.gov.uk
Youth Dance England – www.yde.org.uk
Youth Sport Trust – www.youthsporttrust.org

Other useful links
Coachwise 1st4Sport – www.1st4sport.com
The 24 Hour Museum – www.24hourmuseum.org.uk
PE Scholar – www.pescholar.com
Physical Literacy – www.physical-literacy.org.uk
Sport and Recreation Alliance (formerly CCPR) – www.ccpr.org.uk
Teachernet – www.teachernet.gov.uk

BIBLIOGRAPHY

Alexander, R. (2004) 'Still no pedagogy? Principle, pragmatism and compliance in primary education', *Cambridge Journal of Education*, 34(1): 7–33.

Alexander, R. (2009) *Towards and New Primary Curriculum*, available at: www.primary review.org.uk (accessed 1 January 2014).

Ankers, L. and Dixon, S. (2009) 'Personal learning and thinking skills in Physical Education', *Physical Education Matters*, 4(4): 15–19.

Aristotle (1338) *Politics*, Book 5.3.

Asher, J. (1983) *Learning Another Language Through Action*, Los Angeles, CA: Sky Oaks.

Atter, E. (2008) *Can't Play, Won't Play*, London: Jessica Kingsley.

Avis, J., Fisher, R. and Thompson, R. (eds) (2010) *Teaching in Lifelong Learning: A Guide to Theory and Practice*, Berkshire: McGraw Hill.

Bailey, R. and Macfadyen, T. (2000) *Teaching Physical Education 5–11*, London: Continuum.

Barnes, J. (2007) *Cross-Curricular Learning 3–14*, London: Sage.

Barton, B. (2006) *Safety, Risk and Adventure in Outdoor Activities*, London: Sage.

Becta (2009) *Primary Physical Education with ICT: A Pupil's Entitlement to ICT in Primary Physical Education*, London: Becta.

Bee, H. (2010) *The Developing Child*, New York: Allyn & Bacon.

Beetlestone, F. (1998) *Creative Children, Creative Thinking*, Buckingham: Oxford University Press.

Benn, B., Benn, T. and Maude, P. (2007) *A Practical Guide to Teaching Gymnastics*, Leeds: Coachwise.

Boden, M. (2001) 'Creativity and knowledge', in A. Craft, B. Jeffreys and M. Leibling (eds), *Creativity in Education*, London: Continuum, pp. 95–102.

Bond, K. E. (2001) '"I'm not an eagle, I'm a chicken!": young children's experiences of creative dance', *Early Childhood Connections*, 7(4): 41–51.

Bond, K. and Stinson, S. (2000/2001) '"I feel like I'm going to take off!" Young people's experiences of the superordinary in dance', *Dance Research Journal*, 32(2): 52–87.

Bond, K. and Stinson, S. (2007) '"It's work, work, work, work." Young people's experience of effort and engagement in dance', *Research in Dance Education*, 8(2): 155–83.

Boyd, B. (2005) *Caught in the Headlights: Seeking Permission to be Creative within the Scottish System of Comprehensive Education*, paper presented at ESRC seminar, Documenting Creative Learning, Strathclyde University, October 2005, available at: http://open creativity.open.ac.uk (accessed 1 January 2014).

Bradley, K. (2008) *Rudolph Laban*, London: Routledge.

Brinson, P. (1991) *Dance as Education*, London: Falmer Press.

British Gymnastics (2013) *Schemes and Awards*, available at: www.british-gymnastics.co.uk (accessed 1 January 2014).

British Heart Foundation (2013) *Early Movers*, Loughborough: British Heart Foundation.

Bruner, J. S. (1966) *Toward a Theory of Instruction*, Cambridge, MA: Belknap Press.

Bruner, J. (1983) *Child's Talk: Learning to Use Language*, Oxford: Oxford University Press.

Bursztyn, C. K. (ed.) (2012) *Young Children and the Arts: Nurturing Imagination and Creativity*, Charlotte, NC: Information Age Publishing.

Butler, J. (2005) *Teaching Games for Understanding: Theory, Research and Practice*, Champaign, IL: Human Kinetics.

Campbell, S. (2013) *Mail Online*, 25 May, available at: www.dailymail.co.uk (accessed 1 January 2014).

Chappell, K., Craft, A., Rolfe, L. and Jobbins, V. (2009) 'Dance partners for creativity: choreographing space for co-participative research into creativity and partnership in dance education', *Research in Dance Education*, 10(3): 177–197.

Cheatum, B. (2000) *Physical Activities for Improving Children's Learning and Behaviour*, Champaign, IL: Human Kinetics.

Claxton, G. (1999) *Wise Up: The Challenge of Lifelong Learning*, London: Bloomsbury Publishing

Claxton, G. (2000) 'The anatomy of intuition', in T. Atkinson and G. Claxton (eds), *The Intuitive Practitioner*, Buckingham and Philadelphia, PA: Open University Press, pp. 32–52.

Craft, A. (2000) *Creativity Across the Primary Curriculum: Framing and Developing Practice*, London: Routledge.

Craft, A. (2001) 'Little c creativity', in A. Craft, B. Jeffrey and M. Leibling (eds), *Creativity in Education*, London: Continuum, pp. 45–61.

Craft, A. (2002) *Creativity and Early Years Education*, London: Continuum.

Craft, A. (2005) *Creativity in Schools: Tensions and Dilemmas*, London: Routledge.

Craft, A., Jeffrey, B. and Leibling, M. (2001) *Creativity in Education*, London: Continuum.

Creative Partnerships (2008) *Five Hours a Week of Quality Arts and Culture for Every Child*, available at: www.creative-partnerships.com/offer (accessed 1 January 2014).

Cremin, T. (2009) *Teaching English Creatively*, London: Routledge.

Csikszentmihalyi, M. (1996) *Creativity: Flow and the Psychology of Discovery and Invention*, New York: HarperCollins.

Cullingford, C. (2007) 'Creativity and pupils' experience of school', *Education 3–13: International Journal of Primary, Elementary and Early Years Education*, 35(2): 133–42.

Danks, F. (2009) *Go Wild! 101 Things to Do Outdoors Before You Grow Up*, London: Francis Lincoln.

Danks, F. and Schofield, J. (2006) *Nature's Playground: Activities, Crafts and Games to Encourage Your Children to Enjoy the Great Outdoors*, London: Francis Lincoln.

Danks, F. and Schofield, J. (2012) *The Stick Book: Loads of Things You Can Make or Do with a Stick*, London: Francis Lincoln.

Danks, F. and Schofield, J. (2013) *The Wild Weather Book: Loads of Things to Do Outdoors in Rain, Wind and Snow*, London: Francis Lincoln.

Davies, H. J. (1999) 'Standards in Physical Education in England at Key Stage 1 and 2: past, present and future', *European Review of Physical Education*, 4(2): 173–88.

Davies, M. (2003) *Movement and Dance in Early Childhood*, London: Sage.

Davis, B. and Waite, S. (2005) *Forest Schools: An Evaluation of the Opportunities and Challenges in Early Years*, Final Report, January 2005, Plymouth: University of Plymouth.

Den Duyn, N. (1997) *Game Sense: Developing Thinking Players Workbook*, Canberra: Australian Sports Commission.

Department for Children, Schools and Families (DCSF) (2008) *Statutory Framework for the Early Years Foundation Stage*, London: Department for Children, Schools and Families.

Department for Children, Schools and Families (DCSF) (2013) *Statutory Framework for the National Curriculum*, London: Department for Children, Schools and Families.

Department for Children, Schools and Families (DCSF) and Association for Physical Education (2008) *Physical Education*, London: CfBT.

Department for Culture Media and Sport (DCMS) and Department for Education and Skills (DfES) (2006) *Nurturing Creativity and Young People*, London: HMSO.

Department for Culture, Media and Sport (DCMS) and Department for Education and Skills (DfES) (2007) *Government Response to Nurturing Creativity and Young People*, London: HMSO.

Department for Education (DfE) (2010) *The Importance of Teaching: The Schools White Paper*, London: Department for Education.

Department for Education (DfE) (2011) *Policy Paper: Framework for the National Curriculum: A Report by the Expert Panel for the National Curriculum Review*, London: Department for Education.

Department for Education (DfE) (2013) *The National Curriculum in England Framework Document*, London: Department for Education.

Department for Education and Skills (DfES) (2003) *Excellence and Enjoyment*, London: Department for Education and Skills.

Department for Education and Skills (DfES) (2006) *Learning Outside the Classroom Manifesto*, London: Department for Education and Skills.

Department of Education and Science (DES) (1972) *Movement*, London: HMSO.

Desailly, J. (2012) *Creativity in the Primary Classroom*, London: Sage.

Dillon, J., Morris, M., O'Donnell, L., Reid, A., Rickinson, M. and Scott, W. (2005) *Engaging and Learning with the Outdoors: The Final Report of the Outdoor Classroom in a Rural Context Action Research Project*, Slough: National Foundation for Educational Research.

Doherty, J. and Bailey, R. (2003) *Supporting Physical Development and Physical Education in the Early Years*, Buckingham: Open University Press.

Drew, S. and Atter, E. (2008) *Can't Play, Won't Play*, London: Jessica Kingsley.

Evans, J., Davies, B. and Penney, D. (1996) 'Teachers, teaching and the social construction of gender relations', *Sport, Education and Society*, 1(2): 165–83.

Evans, J., Rich, E., Davies, B. and Allwood, R. (2005) 'The embodiment of learning: what the sociology of education doesn't say about "risk" in going to school', *International Studies in Sociology of Education*, 15(2).

Fedewa, A. L. and Ahn, S. (2011) 'The effects of physical activity and physical fitness on children's cognitive outcomes: a meta-analysis', *Research Quarterly for Exercise and Sport*, 82(3): 521–35.

Feldman, D. H., Csikszentmihalyi, M. and Gardner, H. (1994) *Changing the World: A Framework for the Study of Creativity*, Westport, CT, and London: Praeger.

Fisher, R. and Williams, M. (2004) *Unlocking Creativity in Children*, London: Routledge.

Fjortoft, I. (2004) 'Landscape as playscape: the effects of natural environments on children's play and motor development, *Children, Youth and Environments*, 14(2): 21–44.

Flintoff, A. and Scraton, S. (2001) 'Stepping into active leisure? Young women's perceptions of active lifestyles and their experiences of school Physical Education', *Sport Education and Society*, 6: 5–22.

Flintoff, A. and Scraton, S. (2005) 'Gender and Physical Education', in K. Green and K. Hardman (eds), *Physical Education: Essential Issues*, London: Sage, pp. 161–79.

Frapwell, A. and Caldecott, S. (2011) *In Deep: Learning to Learn*, Worcester: afPE.

Fryer, M. (1996) *Creative Teaching and Learning*, London: Paul Chapman.

Gallahue, D. (1999) *Understanding Motor Development*, New York: McGraw Hill.

Galton, M (2008) *Creative Practitioners in Schools and Classrooms: Final Report of the Project – The Pedagogy of Creative Practitioners in Schools*, London: Creative Partnerships.

Gardner, H. (1993) *Frames of Mind*, London: Fontana.

Giguere, M. (2006) 'Thinking as they create: do children have similar experiences in dance and in language arts?', *Journal of Dance Education*, 6(2): 41–7.

Gilbert, R. (1998) 'Physical Education: the key partner', *British Journal of Physical Education*, 29(1): 18–20.

Gill, T. (2010) *Nothing Ventured . . . Balancing Risks and Benefits in the Outdoors*, available at: www.englishoutdoorcouncil.org/publications (accessed 1 January 2014).

Gladwell, M. (2008) *Outliers*, London: Penguin.

Goddard Blythe, S. (2005) *The Well Balanced Child*, Stroud: Hawthorn Press.

Goddard Blythe, S. (2012) *Assessing Neuromotor Readiness for Learning*, Chichester: Wiley-Blackwell.

Goodwin, P. (2010) *The Literate Classroom*, London: David Fulton.

Gough, M. (1999) *Knowing Dance: A Guide for Creative Teaching*, London: Dance Books.

Grainger, T., Barnes, J. and Scoffham, S. (2004) 'A creative cocktail: creative teaching in initial teacher education', *Journal of Education for Teaching: International Research and Pedagogy*, 30(3): 243–53.

Greenland, P. (1995) *Developmental Movement Play*, Suffolk: JABADO.

Griffin, L. and Butler, J. (eds) (2005) *Teaching Games for Understanding*, Leeds: Human Kinetics.

Griggs, G. (2007) *Physical Education: The Essential Toolkit for Primary School Teachers*, Blackburn: ePrint.

Griggs, G. (ed.) (2012) *An Introduction to Primary Physical Education*, Abingdon: Routledge.

Griggs, G. and McGregor, D. (2012) 'Scaffolding and mediating for creativity: suggestions from reflecting on practice in order to develop the teaching and learning of gymnastics', *Journal of Further and Higher Education*, 36(2): 225–41.

Guildenhuys, C. (1996) 'Movement and second language acquisition', *Sport, Education and Society*, 1(2): 12–16.

Hargreaves, A. (2001) 'Emotional geographies of teaching', *Teachers College Record*, 102: 1056–80.

Harris, J. (2008) *Health Position Paper*, Reading: Association for Physical Education.

Harrison, P. (1998) 'Why Physical Education teachers should reject the new proposals for primary school Physical Education', *British Journal of Physical Education*, 29(1): 4–6.

Harvey, S., Cushion, C. J. and Massa-Gonzalez, A. (2010) 'Learning a new method: Teaching Games for Understanding in the coaches' eyes', *Physical Education and Sport Pedagogy*, 15(4): 361–82.

Hayden-Davies, D. (2005) 'How does the concept physical literacy affect what is and might be the practice of Physical Education?', *British Journal of Teaching Physical Education*, 36(3): 45–8.

Hayden Davies, D. and Whitehead, M. (2010) *Physical Literacy Teaching Styles*, available at: www.physical-literacy.org.uk/Teaching-Styles.pdf (accessed 1 January 2014).

Hoeger, W. and Hoeger, S. (1993) *Fitness and Wellness*, Belmont, VA: Wadsworth.

Hopper, B., Grey, J. and Maude, P. (2000) *Teaching Physical Education in the Primary School*, London: Routledge.

International Physical Literacy Association (IPLA) (2014) Definition of physical literacy, available at: www.physical-literacy.org.uk

Isaacs, S. (1954) *The Educational Value of the Nursery School*, London: British Association of Early Childhood Education.

James, A. and Pollard, M. (2011) *Ten Key Principles of Effective Teaching and Learning*, available at: www.tlrp.org (accessed 1 January 2014).

Jarvis, P., Holford, J. and Griffin, C. (2005) *The Theory and Practice of Learning*, Abingdon: Routledge.

Jeffrey, B. and Craft, A. (2001) 'The universalization of creativity', in A. Craft, B. Jeffrey and M. Leibling (eds), *Creativity in Education*, London: Continuum, pp. 17–34.

Jeffrey, B. (2006) 'Creative teaching and learning: towards a common discourse and practice', *Creativity in Education*, 36(3): 399–414.

Jeffrey, B. and Woods, P. (1997) 'The relevance of creative teaching: pupils' views', in A. Pollard, D. Thieson and A. Filer (eds), *Children and Their Curriculum: Perspectives of Primary and Elementary School Children*, London: Falmer Press, pp. 58–68.

Jeffrey, B. and Woods, P. (1998) *Testing Teachers: The Effects of Inspections on Teachers*, London: Routledge.

Jeffrey, B. and Woods, P. (2003) *The Creative School: A Framework for Success, Quality and Effectiveness*, London: RoutledgeFalmer.

Jeffrey, G. (ed.) (2005) *The Creative College: Building Successful Learning in Culture and the Arts*, London: Trentham Books.

Jiesamfoek, H. (2012) 'Dance and play', in C. K. Bursztyn (ed.), *Young Children and the Arts: Nurturing Imagination and Creativity*, Charlotte, NC: Information Age Publishing, pp. 195–207.

Jones, R. and Wyse, D. (eds) (2004) *Creativity in the Primary Curriculum*, London: David Fulton.

Kaplan, R. and Kaplan, S. (1989) *The Experience of Nature: A Psychological Perspective*, Cambridge: Cambridge University Press.

Keen, M. (1993) 'Early development and attainment of normal gait', *American Academy of Orthotics and Prosthetics*, 5(2).

Kiphard, E. (1995) *Mototherapie*, Dortmund: Borgmann.

Laban, R. (1948) *Modern Educational Dance*, second edition 1963, revised by L. Ullmann, London: MacDonald & Evans.

Laban, R. (1966) *Choreutics*, annotated and edited by L. Ullmann, London: MacDonald & Evans.

Laban, R. (1984) *A Vision of Dynamic Space*, compiled by L. Ullmann, London: The Falmer Press.

Laban, R. (2011) *The Mastery of Movement*, fourth edition, revised by L. Ullmann, Alton: Dance Books.

Lavin, J. (ed.) (2008) *Creative Approaches to Physical Education: Helping Children to Achieve Their True Potential*, Abingdon: Routledge.

Lee, R. (2008) 'Aiming for stewardship not ownership', in D. Amans (ed.), *An Introduction to Community Dance Practice*, London: Palgrave MacMillian.

Lewis, I. (2005) 'Nature and adventure', *ECOS*, 1: 14–19.

Light, R. (2013) *Game Sense*, Abingdon: Routledge.

Light, R. and Fawns, R. (2003) 'Knowing the game: integrating speech and action in games teaching through TGfU, *Quest*, 55(2): 161–76.

Lindqvist, G. (2001) 'The relationship between play and dance', *Research in Dance Education*, 2(1): 41–52.

Loughton, T. (2012) *Speech: Tim Loughton on Promoting PE in Schools*, London: Department for Education, available at: www.gov.uk/government/speeches/tim-loughton-on-promoting-pe-in-schools (accessed 1 January 2014).

Loveless, A. M. (2002) *Literature Review in Creativity, New Technologies and Learning*, Bristol: Futurelab.

Lubart, T. L. (1999) 'Creativity across cultures', in R. J. Sternberg (ed.), *Handbook of Creativity*, Cambridge: Cambridge University Press, pp. 339–50.

Lynn, S. J. and Rhue, J. W. (1986) 'The fantasy-prone person: hypnosis, imagination and creativity', *Journal of Personality and Social Psychology*, 51: 404–8.

Macintyre, C. (2000) *Dyspraxia in the Early Years*, London: David Fulton.

McIntyre, M. (2010) *Lucidity and Science Parts I and II*, available at: www.atm.damtp.cam.ac.uk (accessed 1 January 2014).

McMaster, Sir B. (2008) *Supporting Excellence in the Arts: From Measurement to Judgement*, London: Department for Culture, Media and Sport.

Massey, D. (2004) 'Geographies of responsibility', *Human Geography*, 86(1): 5–18.

Maude, P. (2001) *Physical Children, Active Teaching*, Buckingham: Open University Press.

Maude, P. (2003) *Observing Children Moving*, CD-ROM, Reading: afPE and Tacklesport.

Maude, P. (2007) 'Movement and physical development', *EYE* (*Journal: Early Years Educator*), April 2007, available at: www.earlyyearseducator.co.uk (accessed 1 January 2014).

Maude, P. (2008) 'From movement development into early years Physical Education', in D. Whitebread and P. Coltman (eds), *Teaching and Learning in the Early Years*, third edition, London: Routledge.

Maude, P. (2009) 'How outdoor play develops physical literacy', *EYE* (*Journal: Early Years Educator*), April 2009, available at: www.earlyyearseducator.co.uk (accessed 1 January 2014).

Maude, P. (2010) 'Physical literacy and the young child', in M. E. Whitehead (ed.) *Physical Literacy Throughout the Lifecourse*, London: Routledge.

Maude, P. and Whitehead, M. (2004) *Observing and Analysing Learners' Movement*, CD-ROM, Reading: afPE and Tacklesport.

Millar, S. (1967) *The Psychology of Play*, London: Cox & Syman.

Montessori, M. (1966) *The Secret of Childhood*, New York: Ballantine Books.

Montessori, M. (1996) *The Absorbent Mind*, New York: Holt Paperbacks.

Mooney, R. L. (1963) 'A conceptual model for integrating four approaches to the identification of creative talent', in C. W. Taylor and F. Barren (eds), *Scientific Creativity: Its Recognition and Development*, New York: Wiley, pp. 331–40.

Mosston, M. and Ashworth, S. (1990) *The Spectrum of Teaching Styles: From Command to Discovery*, New York: Longman.

Mosston, M. and Ashworth, S. (2002) *Teaching Physical Education*, fifth edition, San Francisco, CA: Benjamin Cummings.

Nathan, J. (2007) *Oh My Darling, Porcupine*, Minnesota, MN: Meadowbrook Press.

National Advisory Committee on Creative and Cultural Education (NACCCE) (1999) *All Our Futures: Creativity, Culture and Education*, London: National Advisory Committee on Creative and Cultural Education.

NHS (n.d.) *Dyspraxia (Children)*, available at: www.nhs.uk/conditions/Dyspraxia-(childhood)/Pages/Introduction.aspx (accessed 1 January 2014).

O'Brien, L. and Murray, R. (2006) *A Marvellous Opportunity for Children to Learn: The Evaluation of Forest School in England and Wales*, Surrey: Forest Research/Forestry Commission.

Office for Standards in Education (Ofsted) (2003) *Expecting the Unexpected: Developing Creativity in Primary and Secondary Schools*, London: Office for Standards in Education.

Opie, I. and Opie, P. (1969) *Children's Games in Street and Playground*, Oxford: Clarendon Press.

Oxley, J. (1998) 'Never mind literacy and numeracy, what about Physical Education?', *Bulletin of Physical Education*, 29(1): 55–7.

Perry, J. (2001) *Outdoor Play Teaching Strategies with Young Children*, New York: Teachers College Press.

Piaget, J. (1952) *The Origins of Intelligence in Children*, New York: W. W. Norton.

Piaget, J. (1962) *Play, Dreams and Imitation*, available at: www.psych.utoronto.ca/users/peterson/Psy2302011/03Piaget.pdf (accessed 1 January 2014).

Pickard, A. and Earl, J. (2004) 'The potential and possibilities of musical and physical literacies', in P. Goodwin (ed.), *Literacy Through Creativity*, London: David Fulton, pp. 112–23.

Pope, C. (2005) 'Once more with feeling: affect and playing with the TGfU model', *Physical Education and Sport Pedagogy*, 10(3): 271–86.

Prensky, M. (2001) 'Digital natives, digital immigrants', *On the Horizon*, 9(5): 1–6.

Press, C. and Warburton, E. C. (2007) 'Creativity research in dance', in L. Bresler (ed.), *International Handbook of Research in Arts Education*, New York: Kluwer/Springer, pp. 1271–86.

Qualifications and Curriculum Agency (QCA) (2003) *Creativity: Find It, Promote It*, London: Qualifications and Curriculum Agency.

Qualifications and Curriculum Agency (QCA) (2007) 'A framework of personal learning and thinking skills', *PE Matters*, Winter: 15.

Rasberry, C., Lee, S., Robin, L., Laris, B., Russell, L., Coyle, K. and Nihiser, A. (2011) 'The association between school-based physical activity, including Physical Education, and academic performance: a systematic review of the literature', *Preventive Medicine*, 52(1): 10–20.

Ratey, J. and Hagerman, E. (2008) *SPARK: The Revolutionary New Science of Exercise and the Brain*, New York: Little Brown & Company.

Revell, P. (2000) 'Strategic moves', *Sports Teacher*, pp. 14–15.

Robinson, K. (2001) *Out of Our Minds*, Chichester: Capstone.

Ryan, R. M. and Deci, E. L. (2000) 'Intrinsic and extrinsic motivations: classic definitions and new directions', *Contemporary Educational Psychology*, 25: 54–67.

Sacha, T. J. and Ross, S. W. (2006) 'Effect of pretend imagery in learning dance in preschool children', *Early Childhood Education Journal*, 33: 341–5.

Sanders, L (ed.) (2012) *Dance Teaching and Learning: Shaping Practice*, London: Dance England.

Sanders, L. (ed.) (2013) *Dance Teaching and Learning: Shaping Practice*, second edition, London: Youth Dance England.

Shonkoff, J. P. and Phillips, D. A. (eds) (2000) *From Neurons to Neighborhoods: The Science of Early Childhood Development*, Washington, DC: National Academy Press.

Siddall, J. (2010) *Dance in and Beyond Schools*, London: Youth Dance England.

Singer, D. and Singer, J. (2005) *Imagination and Play in the Electronic Age*, Cambridge, MA: Harvard University Press.

Smith-Autard, J. (2002) *The Art of Dance in Education*, second edition, London: A & C Black.

Speednet Survey (2000) 'Primary school Physical Education – Speednet survey makes depressing reading', *British Journal of Physical Education*, 4(2): 173–88.

Sternberg, R. J. (ed.) (1999) *Handbook of Creativity*, Cambridge: Cambridge University Press.

Sternberg, R. J. and Lubart, T. I. (1999) 'The concept of creativity: prospects and paradigms', in R. J. Sternberg (ed.), *Handbook of Creativity*, Cambridge: Cambridge University Press, pp. 3–15.

Stinson, S. (1998) *Dance for Young Children: Finding the Magic in Movement*, Reston, VA: American Alliance for Health, Physical Education, Recreation and Dance.

Taylor, A. F., Wiley, A., Kuo, F. E. and Sullivan, W. C. (1998) 'Growing up in the inner city: green spaces as places to grow', *Environment and Behaviour*, 30: 3–27.

Taylor, P. (1998) *Redcoats and Patriots: Reflective Practice in Drama and Social Studies. Dimensions of Drama*, Portsmouth: Heinemann

Thomas, G. and Thompson, G. (2004) *A Child's Place: Why Environment Matters to Children*, London: Green Alliance and Demos Report.

Thorpe, R., Bunker, B. and Almond, L. (eds) (1986) *Rethinking Games Teaching*, Loughborough: University of Technology.

Tomkins, A. (2012) 'Session planning (part 2 – macro level issues): a planning framework' in L. Sanders (ed.), *Dance Teaching and Learning: Shaping Practice*, London: Youth Dance England, pp. 66–74.

Turner-Bisset, R. (2007) 'Performativity by stealth: a critique of recent initiatives on creativity', *Education 3–13*, 35: 193–203.

Visual Learning Company (2007) *Games Activities* DVD, www.visuallearning.co.uk.

Visual Learning Company (2007) *Gymnastics* DVD, www.visuallearning.co.uk.

Visual Learning Company (2007) *Invasion Games* DVD, www.visuallearning.co.uk.

Visual Learning Company (2007) *Net/Wall, Striking/Fielding Games*, DVD, www.visual learning.co.uk.

Voce, A. (2006) *Play England*, London: Play England.

Vygotsky, L. S. (1978) *Mind and Society: The Development of Higher Mental Processes*, Cambridge, MA: Harvard University Press.

Warburton, P. (2001) 'A sporting future for all: fact or fiction', *British Journal of Teaching Physical Education*, 32(2): 18–21.

Whitehead, M. E. (2001) 'The concept of physical literacy', *European Journal of Physical Education*, 6(2): 127–38.

Whitehead, M. (2009) *Physical Literacy*, available at: www.physical-literacy.org.uk (accessed 1 January 2014).

Whitehead, M. E. (ed.) (2010) *Physical Literacy Throughout the Lifecourse*, London: Routledge.

Whitlam, P. (2012) *Safe Practice in Physical Education*, Reading: AfPE/Coachwise.

Wolpert, D. (2012) 'A moving story', *Cambridge Alumni Magazine*, 66, Easter.

Wood, E. (2009) 'Conceptualizing a pedagogy of play: international perspectives from theory, policy and practice', in D. Kuschner (ed.), *From Children to Red Hatters: Diverse Images and Issues of Play*, New York: University Press of America, pp. 166–90.

Wood, E. and Attfield, J. (2005) *Play, Learning and the Early Childhood Curriculum*, London: Paul Chapman.

Wright, L. (2004) 'Preserving the value of happiness in primary school Physical Education', *Physical Education and Sport Pedagogy*, 9(2): 149–63.

Wyse, D. and Spendlove, D. (2007) 'Partners in creativity: action research and creative partnerships', *Education 3–13*, 35(2): 181–91.

Youth Sport Trust (2012) *Start to Move*, available at: www.starttomovezone.com (accessed 1 January 2014).

INDEX